**Community Care
Practice Handbooks**

General Editor: Martin Davies

Law for Social Workers:
An Introduction

Community Care Practice Handbooks

General Editor: Martin Davies

5 The Essential Social Worker: A Guide to Positive Practice — *Martin Davies*
7 Alcohol Related Problems — *Linda Hunt*
8 Residential Care: A Community Resource — *Leonard Davis*
9 Working with the Elderly — *Eunice Mortimer*
10 Welfare Rights — *Ruth Cohen and Andrée Rushton*
12 Adolescents and Social Workers — *Margaret Crompton*
13 Children In and Out of Care — *Claire Wendelken*
14 Sex and the Social Worker — *Leonard Davis*
15 Consultation — *Allan Brown*
16 Social Work and Health Care — *Andrée Rushton and Penny Davies*
17 Teaching and Learning for Practice — *Barbara Butler and Doreen Elliott*
18 Social Work Practice in Mental Health — *Peter Huxley*
19 The ABC of Child Abuse Work — *Jean G. Moore*
20 The Police and Social Workers — *Terry Thomas*
21 Teaching Practical Social Work — *Hazel Danbury*
22 Working with Depressed Women — *Alison Corob*
23 Contracts in Social Work — *John Corden and Michael Preston-Shoot*
24 An Introduction to Social Work Theory — *David Howe*
25 Working with Drug Users — *Ronno Griffiths and Brian Pearson*
26 Values in Social Work — *Michael Horne*
27 Child Placement: Principles and Practice — *June Thoburn*
28 Mediation in Family Disputes — *Marian Roberts*
29 Social Inquiry Reports — *Anthony Bottoms and Andrew Stelman*
30 Law for Social Workers: An Introduction — *Caroline Ball*

Law for Social Workers: An Introduction

Caroline Ball

WILDWOOD HOUSE

Published by
Wildwood House Limited
Gower House
Croft Road
Aldershot
Hants GU11 3HR
England

Gower Publishing Company
Old Post Road
Brookfield
Vermont 05036
USA

British Library Cataloguing in Publication Data

Ball, Caroline
    Law for Social Workers: an introduction —
    (Community care practice handbooks; v.30)
    1. Great Britain. Welfare work. Law
    I. Title   II. Series
    344.104'313

Library of Congress Cataloging-in-Publication Data

Ball, Caroline, 1938–
    Law for social workers: an introduction
    (Community care practice handbooks; 30)
    Bibliography: p.
    Includes index
    1. Social workers — Legal status, laws, etc. —
Great Britain. I. Title. II. Series.
KD3302.B35 1989   344.41'0313   88-33956
ISBN 0-7045-0588-6   344.104313

ISBN 0 7045 0588 6

Printed in Great Britain by
Billing & Sons Ltd, Worcester

Contents

Table of cases   vii

Table of statutes   ix

Acknowledgements   xi

Introduction   xii

PART I   THE SOCIAL WORKER AS INFORMED ADVISER

1   Nature, sources and administration of law   3

2   An outline of the law regarding family breakdown   13

3   Housing, education, welfare rights and discrimination   25

4   The criminal process   41

PART II   THE LEGAL CONTEXT OF CHILD CARE PRACTICE

Introduction   53

5   Routes into care and emergency procedures   56

6   The child in care or under supervision   69

7   Adoption, custodianship and wardship   75

PART III   THE LEGAL CONTEXT OF WORK WITH OTHER CLIENT GROUPS

8   Aspects of disability: mental disorder, the handicapped and elderly   87

9 Juvenile offenders and the Juvenile Court   101

Bibliography   114

Glossary of legal terms   120

Name index   123

Index   125

Table of Cases

Abbreviations for law reports
A.C.   Law Reports: Appeal Cases
All E.R.   All England Law Reports
Fam.   Law Reports: Family
F.L.R.   Family Law Reports
W.L.R.   Weekly Law Reports

A. v. *Berkshire County Council* [1988] The Times 10.6.88.
A. v. *Liverpool City Council* [1982] A.C. 363.
B. (A Minor) (Wardship: Sterilization) [1987] 2 W.L.R. 1213.
C.B. (A Minor), Re [1981] 1 W.L.R. 379.
Coventry City Council v. *T.* [1986] 2 F.L.R. 301.
Davis v. *Johnson* [1979] A.C. 264.
Dipper v. *Dipper* [1981] Fam. 31.
J. v. *C.* [1970] A.C. 567.
J.J. (A Minor) (Wardship: Committal to Care), Re [1986]
    2 F.L.R. 107.
K.D. (A Minor: Access), Re [1988] Family Law Vol. 17 288.
Lewisham London Borough Council v. *Lewisham Juvenile
    Court Justices* [1980] A.C. 273.
McKenzie v. *McKenzie* [1970] 3 W.L.R. 472.
McLean v. *Nugent* [1979] 1 F.L.R. 26.
O. (A Minor: Access), Re [1984] 2 F.L.R. 716.
O'Neill v. *Williams* [1984] 1 F.L.R 1.
Practice Statement (Judicial Precedent) [1966] 1 W.L.R.
    1234.
Practice Direction [1978] 1 W.L.R. 1123.
Practice Direction [1981] 1 W.L.R. 118.
Practice Direction (Divorce: Welfare Report) [1981]
    1 W.L.R. 1162.
Practice Note [1981] 1 All E.R. 224.
Practice Direction [1986] 2 All E.R. 703.

Practice Direction [1978] 1 All E.R. 1087.

Publhofer v. *London Borough of Hillingdon* [1986] 1 All E.R. 467.

R. v. *Corby Juvenile Court, ex parte M.* [1987] 1 F.L.R. 490.

R. v. *Delany* [1988] The Times 30.8.88.

R. v. *Hereford and Worcester County Council or Another, ex parte Lashford* [1987] 1 F.L.R. 508.

R. v. *Plymouth Juvenile Court, ex parte F.* [1987] 1 F.L.R. 169.

R. v. *West Malling Juvenile Court, ex parte K.* [1986] 2 F.L.R. 405.

Richards v. *Richards* [1984] A.C. 1744.

S. (A Minor) (Adoption or Custodianship), Re [1987] 2 W.L.R. 162.

S. v. *Recorder of Manchester* [1971] A.C. 481.

T. (Minors), Re [1988] The Times 17.6.88.

W. v. *Nottinghamshire County Council* [1982] Fam. 1.

W. v. *L.* [1974] 3 W.L.R. 859.

Table of Statutes

Adoption of Children Act 1926 (repealed)
Adoption Act 1976
Bail Act 1976
Child Abduction Act 1984
Child Care Act 1980
Children Act 1975
Children and Young Persons Act 1933
Children and Young Persons Act 1969
Children and Young Persons (Amendment) Act 1986
Chronically Sick and Disabled Persons Act 1970
Criminal Justice Act 1982
Criminal Justice Act 1988
Criminal Law Act 1977
Disabled Persons (Services, Consultation and Representation)
    Act 1986
Domestic Proceedings and Magistrates' Courts Act 1978
Domestic Violence and Matrimonial Proceedings Act 1976
Education Act 1944
Education Act 1980
Education Act 1981
Family Law Reform Act 1987
Guardianship Act 1973
Guardianship of Minors Act 1971
Health and Social Services and Social Security Adjudications
    Act 1983
Housing (Homeless Persons) Act 1977 (repealed)
Housing Act 1985
Matrimonial Causes Act 1973
Matrimonial Homes Act 1983
Mental Health Act 1959
Mental Health (Amendment) Act 1982 (repealed)
Mental Health Act 1983

National Assistance Act 1948
National Assistance (Amendment) Act 1951
Police and Criminal Evidence Act 1984
Protection from Eviction Act 1977
Social Security Act 1986
Supreme Court Act 1981

Statutory instruments
Adoption Agency Regulations 1983 (No. 1964)
Adoption Rules 1984 (No. 265)
Boarding Out of Children Regulations 1955 (No. 1377)
Magistrates' Courts (Advance Information) Rules 1985 (No. 601)
Magistrates' Courts (Children and Young Persons) Rules 1988 (No. 913)
Mental Health (Hospital Guardianship and Consent to Treatment) Regulations 1983 (No. 893)
Secure Accommodation (No. 2) (Amendment) Regulations 1986 (No. 1591)
Secure Accommodation (No. 2) Regulations 1983 (No. 1018)

Acknowledgements

This book owes much to generations of students on the Social Work Course at the University of East Anglia (UEA), guardians *ad litem* in the region and social workers in a variety of local authorities where I have tried to help practitioners grapple with the legal framework of their practice.

I wish to express profound gratitude to all my social work colleagues at UEA, who are a constant source of stimulation and support, and especially to Martin Davies, for his creative encouragement over the years, and June Thoburn for her expertise in explaining basic principles of child care practice to a lawyer, as well as for the constructive pleasure of joint teaching in this field. Anne Borrett has processed many drafts with humour, skill and patience for which I am deeply grateful.

The Children Bill which introduces major changes in child care law was unfortunately published too late for mention in the text; however the changes it will introduce are of such breadth and complexity that it is very unlikely that any of the new provisions will be implemented for at least a year after the Act reaches the statute book.

The law is stated as it stood on 1 September 1988. The inevitability that changes will have occurred before publication date is a reflection of the complexity of the subject-matter, the organic nature of the law and, in the case of that relating to child care, where change is so long overdue, its vulnerability to political whim. All errors and omissions are entirely my own.

Introduction

Like it or not, there is increasing awareness that most social work takes place in a statutory setting, and that, in order to practise as effective professionals, social workers have not only to be familiar with the nature and extent of their legal powers and duties, but also need to be able to recognize the legal implications of other factors in their clients' lives.

Well over a decade ago the Central Council for Education and Training in Social Work (CCETSW) published the conclusions of the eminent study group which had spent some time considering and recommending the level of legal knowledge necessary for qualified social workers, and an appropriate curriculum for its teaching (CCETSW, 1974). In its report that group first articulated the useful distinction between 'professional law' — i.e. the statutory framework within which social workers function in the field of child care, mental health, the elderly and handicapped, as well as probation officers — and the need for a lesser, but none the less important, level of knowledge of the working of the legal system and the law that affects all citizens. A confident familiarity with the former is an essential ingredient of effective practice (Davies, 1985). In addition, where social workers have some understanding of the latter, which includes such areas as housing or involvement in the criminal or divorce process, clients will benefit from the worker's ability to recognize the legal nature of a problem or situation and advise or refer on accordingly.

Recent research evidence suggests that Certificate of Qualification in Social Work (CQSW) courses are not making adequate provision for law teaching, either in academic or practice terms, and that newly qualified social workers are very unlikely to be confidently, or even at all, familiar with the statutory framework of practice. The report on the teaching and assessment of law in social work education seeks to address the problems and to make recommendations regarding many aspects of law teaching on qualifying and post-qualifying courses (Ball *et al.*, 1988).

In the mid-1970s when the first of a number of social work law texts were published, they mostly covered (more or less adequately) the whole range of professional law and sometimes some 'advisory' law as well. During the past decade, however, social workers' awareness of the need for detailed knowledge of their statutory powers and duties has developed at almost the same pace as the complexity of child care law. Not only that, but the provisions of the Mental Health Act 1983 have given approved social workers increased powers and duties and hence a greater obligation to be familiar with the statutory framework within which they practise.

The effect of this is that in the specialist professional areas of child care and mental health, a generic law book is no longer adequate; advanced students and experienced workers now require individual specialist texts on professional law, as well as separate guidance on general topics. However, for students and practitioners with little previous legal knowledge, and possibly some antipathy to the subject, it is felt that an introductory text, which aims to aid understanding of the legal context of social work practice and to provide further references where appropriate, would be useful. This is the role which this book is intended to play.

PART I
THE SOCIAL WORKER AS
INFORMED ADVISER

1 Nature, sources and administration of law

The law, by which is meant the body of rules whereby a civilized society maintains order and regulates its internal affairs as between one individual and another, and between individuals and the state, consists in the UK of common law, statute law (Acts of Parliament) and case law, or judicial precedent. For historical reasons the law of England and Wales profoundly differs from that of Scotland, and in important respects, particularly as regards children and young persons, from that of Northern Ireland; any reference to particular provisions therefore relate only to England and Wales unless the contrary is stated.

Parliament can, by statute, make or change the law in any way that a majority decision of both the House of Commons and the House of Lords, following established procedure, deems appropriate. The judges of the superior courts through their interpretation of statutory provisions and legal principles both define and refine existing law, and may, on occasions, where there is no similar case or established legal principle to which they can refer, make new law. Where judges do 'make' law in this way, Parliament may always, by statute, subsequently restate the law to its own liking. The process of legislation from political or practical ideas through the democratic process to enacted statute is a familiar one, the interpreting and occasional making of law by the judges may be less so.

In order to understand the working of judicial precedent it is necessary to look at the structure of the courts and the way in which decisions in the superior courts have to be followed by those below them in the hierarchy (Figures 1 and 2). The courts within which the law is administered reflect the essential difference between the civil and criminal law. Civil law, for the most part, involves disputes between

European Court

HOUSE OF LORDS

COURT OF APPEAL
CRIMINAL DIVISION

CROWN COURT
HIGH COURT: JUDGE AND JURY

Superior
courts

CROWN COURT
CIRCUIT JUDGE OR RECORDER AND JURY

MAGISTRATES' COURT   Juvenile Court

Inferior
courts

Figure 1   The criminal courts

European Court

HOUSE OF LORDS

COURT OF APPEAL
CIVIL DIVISION

DIVISIONAL COURT OF THE HIGH COURT

HIGH COURT
Queen's Bench, Family, Chancery,
Admiralty and Specialist Divisions

Superior
courts

COUNTY COURT

MAGISTRATES' DOMESTIC COURT   Juvenile Court

Inferior
courts

Figure 2   The civil courts

individual parties, with one seeking either an order, or compensation for loss or damage suffered, against another. The criminal law is concerned with the trial and punishment of those who have acted in a way that is unlawful; this includes, of course, besides acts generally recognized as crimes such as murder, rape and theft, a vast range of matters, such as minor motoring offences, which are only technically 'criminal' in nature but none the less come within the jurisdiction of the criminal courts.

As can be seen from the figures, the separate systems of courts for the administration of the criminal and civil law come together only at the extremities of the jurisdiction of the Juvenile Court and on the occasions in which an appeal reaches the House of Lords, or more rarely the European Court.

Judicial precedent — the system by which the decisions of superior courts are binding on those below them in the hierarchy — not only clarifies and refines the law, but makes it more certain. Where a point of law has been decided in a previous case, a court subsequently hearing a case involving the same point will be bound to follow that decision or differentiate the circumstances of the current case.

A point of law decided in a case in the House of Lords is binding on all other courts below — but not necessarily on itself on a future occasion (Practice Statement (Judicial Precedent) 1966). Decisions in either division of the Court of Appeal bind all the courts below and will generally be followed in their own subsequent decisions. In the High Court, divisional court decisions are binding on judges sitting alone, but one High Court judge's decision will not necessarily be binding — although it is likely to be influential — on another.

The inferior courts, which are the County Court, lower tier of the Crown Court and all the Magistrates' Courts are bound by the decisions of all superior courts, but not by their own or those of other inferior courts.

Information on all important judicial decisions is recorded in reports in which the facts of the case, the points of law involved and the decision are recorded and published according to the specialist subject-matter involved. There is an elaborate system of referencing to enable lawyers and courts to keep track of developments in case law and to trace decisions relevant to particular situations or legal principles (see Glossary).

Jurisdiction of the courts

The civil courts

The venue for civil trials will depend either on the nature of the dispute or the sum of money involved, or sometimes both. As an example, it may be helpful to look first at family proceedings and then at other civil disputes.

One of the complicating factors about child care and family law is that in many proceedings, though not in divorces which cannot be heard by the magistrates, the Domestic Court, the County Court and the High Court have concurrent jurisdiction. It may be a matter of chance, or more probably of a solicitor's preference, whether proceedings such as adoption or custodianship, for instance, are heard in the Domestic Court or the County Court, although as a matter of principle legal aid is only available for the least expensive proceedings which will provide the required order or remedy. Again, mainly on account of the cost, apart from some wardship applications, only the most complex cases go to the Family Division of the High Court. We look at in greater detail family and matrimonial proceedings, in outline, in Chapter 2, and child care proceedings are considered in Chapters 5–7.

Cases such as those involving claims for personal injury or breach of contract will be heard in the County Court if the amount claimed is less than the current ceiling for that court, and in the Queen's Bench Division of the High Court if the amount is greater. Almost all these cases are eventually settled between the parties before the case actually reaches the court, or when it is part-heard.

Appeals from the Magistrates' Domestic Court go to the Family Division of the High Court and from the County and High Courts to the Court of Appeal Civil Division. From there they may, with leave, go to the House of Lords and the European Court. Confusingly, because of their quasi-criminal nature, appeals against the Juvenile Court's decisions in care proceedings are currently heard in the Crown Court.

Criminal courts

All criminal cases concerning adults (aged 17 years and over) start in the Magistrates' Court and most are dealt with there. More serious cases, or those in which the defendant has a right to, and elects, trial by jury will be committed to the Crown Court for trial. Except in inner London and other metropolitan areas where paid and legally qualified stipendary magistrates sit alone, the Magistrates' Courts are staffed by unpaid lay justices, appointed by a process which has in the past often seemed somewhat secretive to the local community. Recently the Lord Chancellor has indicated that such appointments are to be made more openly.

In the Magistrates' Court the justices, usually a chairman and two others, sit with a clerk whose role is to administer the court and advise on the law and other related legal issues such as evidence and procedure. The justices are responsible for all decisions whether they relate to the facts, the law or sentence, and these can be appealed against to the Crown Court, or on a point of law only to the Divisional Court.

About 95 per cent of all criminal cases begin and end with the magistrates; however, in more serious cases the justices will have to decide whether to commit to the Crown Court on bail or to remand the defendant in custody to await trial. Cases committed to the Crown Court will generally be heard in the second tier by a circuit judge or a recorder, possibly sitting with two lay justices and, if the defendant is pleading not guilty, a jury of twelve laymen whose role is to determine guilt or innocence. Murder and some other very serious or complex cases will be heard in the top tier of the Crown Court by a High Court judge, again sitting with a jury if the offence is denied.

Appeals against findings of guilt, or against sentences imposed by the magistrates, are heard in the Crown Court. Those from the Crown Court, against sentence or on a point of law, but not generally against the jury's finding of guilt unless that can be seen to be perverse in view of the judge's summing up of the evidence, are heard by the Criminal Division of the Court of Appeal. On a point of law only, and with the leave of the court, there may be a further appeal to the House of Lords and possibly afterwards to the European Court. (The criminal jurisdiction of the Juvenile Court is considered in greater detail in Chapter 9.)

Access to legal advice and representation
The legal profession is currently divided into two fairly
rigidly separated branches. Various attempts have been made
to fuse aspects of their work but currently solicitors have a
monopoly of direct access to clients and as a general rule
only barristers have a right to be heard in the superior courts.
Although some solicitors specialize in representing their
clients in the courts to which they have access, most of
their work is outside the courts, and most barristers do
mainly advocacy work.

In order to help the public, most of whom will have
occasion to seek professional legal advice only rarely, in their
choice of a solicitor suitable to their needs the Law Society
publishes lists of firms and legal advice centres, indicating
their areas of expertise and whether they undertake legal aid
work. Importantly, they have also established a child care
panel whose members have specialist knowledge and
experience and should be chosen for care and related proceedings in which the law is particularly complex, and good
representation essential.

Legal aid
The legal aid scheme was designed to ensure that access to
the law, by way of advice and where necessary representation, is available to those unable to afford to pay for it
themselves. Basically there are four types of legal aid in
addition to the free duty solicitor scheme which operates
in the criminal courts: legal advice and basic assistance under
the 'green form' scheme, assistance by way of representation,
criminal legal aid and civil legal aid. They depend on separate
financial conditions, though the same basic principles apply,
namely that the granting of legal aid is dependent on the
reasonableness of the client's claim for the service and on
his/her means, in terms of disposable income and capital,
on which liability to pay, at all, in part, or in full, will be
assessed (Moeran, 1982). Current administration of the
scheme and government attempts to limit spending effectively limit entitlement to legal aid to those on very low
incomes.

Under the so-called 'green form' scheme, those who
qualify financially are entitled to a variety of advice and basic
help from a solicitor up to a cost of (currently) £50 or £90

for a petitioner for an undefended divorce or judicial separation. Assistance by way of representative covers the cost of a solicitor preparing a case and representing a party in most proceedings in Magistrates' Domestic Courts. It is also available to patients appearing before Mental Health Review Tribunals.

Legal aid for criminal proceedings is granted by the clerk to the justices in the Magistrates' Court on the basis of the defendant's means and the desirability of his/her being legally represented in the interests of justice, as defined by the criteria laid down by a committee chaired by Lord Widgery (HMSO, 1966). If the clerk to whom application is made considers refusing legal aid, he must put the matter to a magistrate for a decision, subject to the general rule that doubts should be resolved in the defendant's favour. Annually published statistics show an enormous discrepancy between the refusal rates of different courts.

Legal aid for civil proceedings will cover all work leading up to and including representation in court proceedings, by a barrister if necessary. Civil legal aid is not available for cases covered by assistance by way of representation, or for the Coroner's Court, or most tribunals, though it is available for those appearing before employment appeal tribunals. The success of an application, which must be made by a solicitor to the legal aid office local committee, will depend on the applicant's financial eligibility, as assessed by the DHSS, and the committee's view of the reasonableness of the case. Even if eligible for legal aid, litigants may be required to make substantial contributions towards the cost of their representation and, if successful, will have to reimburse the fund.

Support for unrepresented clients
Any litigant in criminal or civil proceedings who is not legally represented may have the assistance of someone, whether legally qualified or not, to sit beside him/her in court, taking notes, offering advice and suggesting questions to be asked. The 'McKenzie man', or woman, so-called after the case in which the Court of Appeal established the concept (*McKenzie* v. *McKenzie* [1970]), may not address the court, but may offer all other advice and assistance. This may be an important role for a social worker to play for an inarticulate client who has been refused legal aid.

Standard of proof, rules of evidence and natural justice

Since possibly liberty, and certainly reputation, may be at stake, a higher standard of proof is required for a conviction in criminal proceedings than for that in civil proceedings. Fashions change and, in criminal cases, there was for a few years a swing away from the generally accepted formula that the court should be 'satisfied beyond reasonable doubt' of the defendant's guilt to the court being 'sure' of it. (More recently, 'reasonable doubt' appears to have found favour again.) However phrased, it is clearly a higher standard than that in civil proceedings, where the issue is one between theoretically equal parties and the court is therefore required to base its decision only on a balance of probabilities in favour of one side or the other.

The law of evidence is for the most part detailed, highly complex and inextricably interwoven with the procedural rules for different proceedings – and best left to lawyers. However, as social workers are often called on to give evidence in court, the basic principles and the extent to which the effective presentation of relevant facts often determines the outcome of care and related proceedings make it essential that social workers have some understanding of the nature of evidence, and of two of the basic rules – i.e. those against hearsay evidence and the asking of leading questions.

Evidence in court consists of the testimony of witnesses given under oath and subject to cross-examination and, subject to many procedural safeguards, the contents of some documents. The rules which exclude certain testimony and documents generally hinge on the principle that evidence must be the best available and must be reliable.

Hearsay, that is the evidence of a statement made by a person who is not giving evidence, in the attempt to establish the truth of what was said, is excluded both on grounds of not being the best available and not being reliable, in that it is not subject to cross-examination. If the truth of that statement is to be established, then the person who made it must be called to give evidence as to what they said. There are many practical exceptions to the rule against hearsay – e.g. it has to be relaxed in regard to social inquiry and similar reports.

Leading questions are not, contrary to popular belief, ones

the answers to which might prove embarrassing or incriminating, but those which suggest the answer required. In order that witnesses give their own evidence and are not led into making the statements that their advocate might want them to make, leading questions may only be asked of witnesses giving their own testimony when the facts are not in dispute. They may be used in cross-examination because the nature of this is to test the accuracy of evidence already given under oath.

Tribunals

There is a large number of administrative tribunals, such as Mental Health Review Tribunals and Social Security Appeals Tribunals, which exercise a quasi-judicial function outside the court system. Mainly these tribunals exist to determine appeals from administrative decisions and are mostly staffed by experts in the particular field, or by lay people representing the community, generally with a legally qualified chairperson. Proceedings are less formal than in courts and legal aid is not normally available for representation. This is therefore an area in which social workers and volunteers can play an important role. Although they are not courts of law, tribunals may possess case law of their own which they follow and they are, in any event, bound by the rules of natural justice (see below).

The Ombudsman

The terms of reference of the Ombudsman — properly the Parliamentary Commissioner for Administration — are to investigate complaints by individuals or corporate bodies who claim to have sustained injustice in consequence of maladministration. In practice, individuals can only approach the Ombudsman through their Member of Parliament. The Ombudsman possesses wide investigatory powers and, although he cannot alter or rescind decisions, as a result of his investigations departments very often take such action or make *ex gratia* payment of compensation.

Complaints about the National Health Service are investigated by the Health Service Commissioner, and against maladministration by local authorities by three Local Commissioners for Administration (Street and Brazier, 1986).

Natural justice

The rules of natural justice provide minimal standards for fair decision-making; these apply not only in courts and tribunals, but also to any public bodies who are under a duty to act judicially. This duty to act fairly in a judicial role is founded on two principles: the rule against bias, for instance, direct financial proprietary interest in the outcome of proceedings or knowledge of one of the litigants which might distort judgement, and the right to a fair hearing, encapsulated in the Latin tag, *audi alterem partem* ('hear both sides equally'). If a breach of natural justice can be established, the injured party is granted leave to seek redress, through judicial review by the High Court, of the proceedings in which the unfair treatment is alleged to have occurred (Ball, 1987d).

The case of *R.* v. *West Malling Juvenile Court, ex parte K.* [1986] provides an example of a remedy for a breach of natural justice.

> Care proceedings were initiated by the local authority in respect of three children who had been looked after by their father, with considerable social work help, for three years after the death of his wife. Separate representation was ordered and a guardian ad litem (GAL) appointed. The father's solicitor tried unsuccessfully to obtain details of any allegations made against the father before the hearing. On the morning of the hearing copies of the welfare and GAL's reports, which made serious allegations concerning the father's care of the children, were served on his advisers. They wished for time to prepare their case and call further evidence to rebut the allegations. The magistrates refused application for an adjournment and proceeded with the hearing. Care orders were made in respect of each child. The father successfully appealed by way of judicial review to quash the care orders on the grounds that he had good reason to feel that he had not had a fair hearing because the justices had refused an adjournment to allow him to prepare a response to the allegations made in the reports.

2 An outline of the law regarding family breakdown

When a marriage breaks down, the relief sought will largely determine the nature of the legal proceedings. Permanent dissolution of a valid marriage, when both parties are still living, can be achieved only by divorce proceedings, though a marriage suffering from a fundamental defect, such as non-consummation, may be annulled. In other proceedings orders may be made which relate to the parties or children of a marriage or, in some circumstances, to cohabitees. The law relating to marriage and the family is both wide in its scope and complex in nature; this chapter gives only a brief introduction and for further detail it will be necessary to consult a specialist textbook (Cretney, 1984; Bromley and Lowe, 1987).

Divorce

A marriage can be terminated only by death or by a decree of divorce or nullity. All suits for divorce are commenced by a petition presented to a Divorce County Court, and almost all will be concluded there; cases may be transferred to the High Court if their complexity, difficulty or gravity justify the move (Practice Direction 1987).

Legal aid was withdrawn from almost all undefended divorce proceedings in 1977, although it is available to make or oppose an application for an injunction, financial relief or an order in relation to children. Petitioners have therefore to draft their own petition and take all the further steps, or pay a solicitor. If petitioners qualify financially, they may be entitled to free legal advice under the 'green-form' scheme up to £90 in value which could provide assistance with form-filling. Printed forms of petition are available from law stationers and court staff are also helpful to unrepresented parties.

No petition may be presented within the first year of marriage, though one presented after that may be based on events which occurred during the first year. Under the Matrimonial Causes Act 1973, the sole ground for divorce is that the marriage has irretrievably broken down; this can only be established by proving one of the five grounds set out in section 1 of the Act:

1. that the respondent has committed adultery and that the petitioner finds it intolerable to live with the respondent;
2. that the respondent has behaved in such a way that the petitioner cannot be expected to live with the respondent;
3. that the respondent has deserted the petitioner; and that this has been for a continuous period of 2 years;
4. that the parties have lived apart for a continuous period of at least 2 years, and that the respondent consents to the decree being granted;
5. that the parties have lived apart for a continuous period of at least 5 years immediately preceding the presentation of the petition.

Although the consent of the respondent is not required, the decree may be withheld if it can be shown that to grant it would cause grave financial or other hardship.

When the petition is served on the respondent, it must be accompanied by two forms, one sets out the steps to be taken and the consequences of a decree and the other is a form of acknowledgement of service which asks the respondent whether the proceedings are going to be defended. If the respondent wishes to defend the proceedings, he/she must file an answer within 29 days of receiving the petition and then the case will be heard in open court.

Under what is called the 'special procedure' — in fact the normal procedure in undefended cases — neither party needs attend court. The petitioner has to make a written application for directions for trial accompanied by an affidavit verifying the facts set out in the petition, any corroborative evidence relied on and certain other information. The registrar enters the cause in the special procedure list and, provided that he is satisfied that the petitioner has proved his/her case and is entitled to a decree, this will be certified and a date fixed on which the judge will announce the decree nisi in open court.

Subject to the court being satisfied as to the welfare of any children of the family, and in certain circumstances as to financial protection for the respondent, the petitioner may apply after 6 weeks (or any shorter time fixed by the court) for the decree to be made absolute. If the petitioner does not apply, the respondent may do so after 3 months from the earliest date on which the petitioner could have applied. Once the decree is absolute (but not before), the marriage is at an end and either party may remarry.

In addition to granting the divorce decree, the court may make a wide range of orders regarding finance and property, and it must before granting a decree absolute make a declaration of satisfaction to the effect that the arrangements for the welfare of every child of the family are 'satisfactory or the best that can be devised in the circumstances', or that it is impracticable for such arrangements to be made (Matrimonial Causes Act 1973, s.41; see also p. 17).

Domestic proceedings in Magistrates' Courts
The Magistrates' Domestic Court has jurisdiction in a number of proceedings relating to marriage breakdown, but not in divorce. The court provides an inexpensive local forum of infinitely variable quality. Assistance by way of representation through the legal aid scheme covers the cost of a solicitor preparing a case and representing a party in most cases in Magistrates' Domestic Courts.

Financial provision
Under section 1 of the Magistrates' Courts and Domestic Proceedings Act 1978, the spouse whose husband has failed to maintain her and the children properly, or has behaved in such a way that she cannot be expected to live with him or has deserted her, can seek:

(a) an order making financial provision;
(b) the court's approval of agreed arrangements;
(c) confirmation of a level of payment which has been made voluntarily for the past 3 months.

The order may be for both periodical and lump-sum payments (not exceeding £500).

Children
Where financial provision is sought, the court must not
dismiss the application or make a final order until it has
decided whether to exercise its powers to make orders for
legal custody, access and maintenance in respect of any child
of the family as defined in the Matrimonial Causes Act 1973
(s.52(1)) (see p. 17).

In 'exceptional circumstances' the court may, in addition
to making an order for custody, access or maintenance, make
a supervision order, committing the child to the care of the
local authority. Care and supervision orders made in matrimonial proceedings have recently been the subject of scrutiny
by the Law Commission (1987a, 1987b).

Applications under the Guardianship of Minors Act 1971 and the Guardianship Act 1973

These proceedings may be heard in the Magistrates' Domestic
Court, the County Court or the High Court. The 1971 Act
enables the father or mother of a child who may or may not
have been married to each other, but are no longer living
together, to apply to the court for orders regarding legal
custody, access and maintenance. The court's decision will
be determined according to the criteria laid down in section 1
of the 1971 Act (see p. 18). Applications for either custody
or financial orders under these Acts are confined to the
parents, although the parents of a deceased parent may apply
for access to their grandchild; and under section 14(a) of
the 1971 Act, *any* grandparent can apply once an order for
legal custody has been made.

Although otherwise excluded under this Act, grandparents
and other relatives may be eligible to apply for legal custody
of the child in custodianship proceedings (see Chapter 7).
Or they may be able to make a child a ward of court and seek
care and control.

Under section 85(7) of the Children Act 1975, only the
mother of an illegitimate child has parental rights and duties
in relation to the child. The Guardianship of Minors Act
1971 enables the father of an illegitimate child to apply for
custody or access to his child, provided that he can prove
paternity. If paternity is disputed, that issue must be resolved
before the court can consider the merits of the application
(*Re O. (A Minor: Access)* [1984]).

Until section 4 of the Family Law Reform Act 1987 is implemented, an application for custody under the 1971 Act provides the only means apart from wardship whereby an unmarried father can gain any parental rights over his children. Even when the 1987 Act is fully implemented, an unmarried father will have to apply to the court for parental rights (Ball, 1988b). As in divorce and domestic proceedings in the Magistrates' Courts, in 'exceptional circumstances', the court may commit the child to the care of the local authority or make a supervision order.

Parents still living together who are in dispute about a particular issue in regard to their children, for instance, the school which they should attend, may apply to the court for its directions under the 1973 Act, and the court may make such order as it thinks proper having regard to the welfare of the child.

Children of the family

A court hearing divorce, nullity or judicial separation proceedings may make such orders as it sees fit for the 'custody and education' of any child of the family under 18 years, whether or not it also grants the decree. Legal custody is defined in the Children Act 1975 as 'so much of the parental rights and duties as relate to the person of the child (including the place and manner in which his time is spent)', but no equivalent definition exists in the divorce legislation and the Court of Appeal has suggested that the custodial parent does not have sole right to make decisions about major issues in the child's life (*Dipper* v. *Dipper* [1981]).

'Child of the family', in relation to parties to a marriage, is defined in the 1973 Act and has the same meaning in Magistrates' Court domestic proceedings, namely one who is under 16 years or older and still in education or training and is:

(a) a child of both parties; and
(b) any other child, not being a child who has been boarded out with those parties by the local authority or voluntary organisation, who has been treated by both of these parties as a child of their family. (s.52(1))

In reaching any decision regarding children in matrimonial and domestic proceedings the court must apply the welfare principle laid down in section 1 of the Guardianship of Minors Act 1971:

Where in any proceedings before any court —

(a) the legal custody or upbringing of a child; or

(b) the administration of any property belonging to or held on trust for a child, or the application of the income thereof, is in question, the court, in deciding that question, *shall regard the welfare of the child as the first and paramount consideration* and shall not take into consideration whether from any other point of view the claim of the father in respect of such legal custody, upbringing, administration or application is superior to that of the mother, or the claim of the mother is superior to that of the father. (Emphasis added.)

This means that in cases directly concerning the child's custody, upbringing or the administration of his/her property the child's interest is paramount; in other related issues it may be important but not the first and only consideration.

Court welfare officers

The probation service provides court welfare teams made up of probation officers who work for a period of time in this role, to service all levels of courts with a family jurisdiction (Murch, 1980). In order to help it reach a decision regarding children the court may at any time request a court welfare officer's report, whether or not custody of the children is being contested. The court may specify the issues it wishes to see addressed in the report, but this should not inhibit the inclusion of any other matters the welfare officer thinks that the court should consider (Practice Direction (Divorce: Welfare Report) 1981) (see Stone, 1989). A recent study of the work of Divorce Court welfare officers provides useful and sensitive comment on the management of services for families caught up in marital breakdown and divorce (Clulow and Vincent, 1987).

Orders which may be made in regard to children

1. *Custody to one spouse, access to the other*   In at least 75 per cent of cases, this means custody to the mother with reasonable or, if parties are unable to agree, defined access to the father. In extreme cases, this may be

supervised by a court welfare officer or local authority
social worker.

2. *Custody to one spouse, care and control to the other*
Such split orders are rarely made and the judicial view is
that they are generally undesirable (*Dipper* v. *Dipper*
[1981]).

3. *Custody to third parties*   In divorce proceedings third
parties, such as grandparents, may 'intervene' to apply
for custody. In Magistrates' Courts matrimonial proceedings, and Guardianship of Minors Act proceedings, third
parties wishing to apply for custody may be regarded as if
they had been qualified to apply, and had applied for,
custodianship under the Children Act 1975 (see Chapter
7).

The matrimonial home

1. *Ownership* and rights on dissolution of a marriage are
technical, complex and beyond the scope of this book;
for a lucid explanation, see Bromley and Lowe (1987,
ch. 4).

2. *Occupation*   It is often the right to occupy the matrimonial or joint home that is critical at the time a
relationship breaks down. If both spouses or partners
have a beneficial interest in the home, for instance, as
co-owners or joint tenants, they have equal rights of
occupation. If only one has a beneficial interest, the
position of a spouse without legal title is more secure
than that of a cohabitee, who none the less may have
some protection; each need separate consideration.

*Spouse's right to occupy a home, in which only one spouse
has a legal title*   Under section 1(1) of the Matrimonial
Homes Act 1983, it is stated:

Where one spouse is entitled to occupy a dwelling house . . . and the
other spouse is not so entitled . . . the spouse not so entitled shall
have the following rights of occupation:

(a) if in occupation, a right not to be evicted or excluded from the
dwelling house or any part thereof except with the leave of
the court given by an order under this section;

(b) if not in occupation, a right with the leave of the court so given
to enter into and occupy the dwelling house.

The applicant spouse's rights under the Act are dependent on:

(i)   the marriage still being in existence;
(ii) the entitled spouse having a legal right to occupy.

Cohabitee's right to occupy   A cohabitee without legal title may be protected if they can establish:

(i)   a contractual licence, by virtue of an interest they may have given up which may amount to consideration;
(ii) a licence by estoppel if the other party has acted in such a way as to be estopped from denying the existence of the right of occupancy;
(iii) otherwise a cohabitee will only have a bare licence and the owner of the premises may recover possession after giving reasonable notice to quit.

Excluding a party from occupation   For this, see below, p. 21.

Domestic violence
Legal protection for victims of domestic violence, adults or children, are contained in a hotchpotch of statutory provision. Child care law (Chapter 6) provides state protection for a child at risk from both parents; the domestic violence provisions concern the protection of partners and of children for whom one partner could provide a safe home if the other were excluded. The main issues are accommodation and personal protection. Varying remedies and levels of protection are available under a number of different statutory provisions, as follows.

Accommodation
Under the Housing Act 1985, Part III (Homeless Persons), a person who has left accommodation as a result of actual or threatened violence to her or her children is not regarded as intentionally homeless and may qualify for full and permanent rehousing if they have a priority need, or for lesser assistance.

The Matrimonial Homes Act 1983 gives the High Court or County Court power to make orders relating to the rights of occupation of all spouses. If one spouse has a right of occupation under section 1(1) of the Act, the court may make an order:

(a) declaring, enforcing or restricting the exercise of that right;
(b) prohibiting, suspending or restricting the exercise by either spouse of the right to occupy the home;
(c) requiring either spouse to permit the other to exercise that right.

Orders under the Act may relate to only part of the premises; require the party in occupation to pay, for instance, repairs and rent or mortgage repayments; and be for a limited period of time, or an interim order pending divorce or the finding of alternative accommodation.

Under the Domestic Violence and Matrimonial Proceedings Act 1976, the County Court has power to grant injunctions to either spouses or cohabitees which may exclude the other party from the whole or part of the matrimonial home; or require the other party to permit the applicant to enter and remain in the whole or part of the matrimonial home. This Act is of particular importance to cohabitees who are not protected under the Matrimonial Homes Act 1983. In the case of *Davis* v. *Johnson* [1979], it was held that a joint tenant could be excluded from premises in favour of his partner.

Spouses may seek remedies only under section 16 of the Domestic Proceedings and Magistrates' Courts Act 1978, which provides that on proof of use, or threatened use, of violence a Magistrates' Domestic Court may make an order requiring a respondent spouse to leave the matrimonial home. It may also make an order requiring the occupant to permit the applicant to enter and remain.

The availability of remedy to non-spouses rests in resort being made more often to the County Court jurisdiction under the 1976 Act than to the Domestic Court. Exclusion of either party from a joint home is a draconian power. The Court of Appeal has given guidance on criteria for the making and length of ouster orders:

(a) *Children's needs* The welfare of children will be one

and often an important factor but is not 'the first and paramount' criteria (*Richards* v. *Richards* [1984]).
(b) *The conduct of the parties*   This must be such as to justify refusal of one to live with the other. Violence would be a justification, tension or mere dislike would probably not (*Richards* v. *Richards* [1984]).
(c) *Parties' needs and resources*   Particularly the ability to find other accommodation including the strength and likely success of claims for re-housing by the housing authority.
(d) *Other considerations*   These include the possibility of a reconciliation; the length of time the parties have lived apart; the imminence of matrimonial proceedings.

Proceedings under the 1976 and 1978 Acts are only intended to provide short-term remedies; 3 months should normally be the limit (Practice Direction 1978).

Personal protection
Criminal proceedings are rarely brought in cases of domestic violence, although they may increase following implementation of the Police and Criminal Evidence Act 1984, which makes one spouse a compellable witness against another unless they are jointly charged. Compensation can now be obtained from the Criminal Injuries Compensation Board in such cases but the success of applications is dependent on satisfying strict qualifying conditions (HMSO, 1986).
   Rather than prosecution of the perpetrator or compensation for injury, the need is usually for protection for the victim and other members of the family. This may be obtained by *judicial separation* on the basis of one of the 'five facts' on which divorce petitions are founded but without the need to establish irretrievable breakdown or by means   of an injunction. A decree of judicial separation relieves the petitioner from the duty of cohabiting with the respondent and orders may be made regarding the custody and welfare of children and financial relief.

Injunctions
Where any non-molestation orders, matrimonial or other related proceedings are pending in the High Court or County Court, an injunction may be sought restraining one spouse,

usually the husband, from molesting, assaulting or otherwise interfering with the wife and children. The County Court has power under the Domestic Violence and Matrimonial Proceedings Act 1976 to grant an injunction on the application of either party to a marriage or a cohabitee, whether or not they are seeking other relief. The injunction may restrain the respondent from molesting the applicant or a child living with the applicant, and exclude him from the home or compel him to admit the applicant to the home. Molestation includes all forms of physical interference and pestering, following about, abusive letters and phone calls, etc. Although all children under age 18 come within the definition, it is doubtful whether an adult son or daughter being molested by the defendant would be protected under the Act (Bromley and Lowe, 1987, p. 162).

An injunction is a powerful order non-compliance with which amounts to contempt of court and puts the party in default at risk of imprisonment. Injunctions are only used by the courts as a last resort. Where danger of serious injury or irreparable damage is real and immediate, an injunction may be granted *ex parte*.

An applicant who has been forced to leave the matrimonial home before taking legal action can apply, provided the violence took place while the parties were living together. The more recent the incident, the more likely the relief (*McLean* v. *Nugent* [1979], and *O'Neill* v. *Williams* [1984]). In the High Court injunctions containing any of the above provisions may be sought independently of other proceedings (Supreme Court Act 1981, s.37, RSC Order 90).

Power of arrest
Committing a party in default to prison requires their apprehension and presence before the court. This may take some time to achieve and leave a spouse or partner in danger of attack. To avoid this, section 2 of the 1976 Act provides that a power of arrest may be attached whenever injunctions are granted restraining the defendant from using violence against the applicant, or a child living with the applicant, or excluding him from the matrimonial home or the area surrounding it. The power can be attached only if the person has in the past caused actual bodily harm to the applicant or child concerned and the court considers it likely to happen

again. The circumstances in which a power of arrest may be attached are even more limited than those in which injunctions may be granted and should normally be limited to 3 months' duration (Practice Notice 1981).

Where there is a power of arrest, any constable may arrest the defendant if there is reasonable cause for suspecting that he is in breach of an injunction. Once arrested, the defendant must be brought before a judge within 24 hours (excluding Sundays, Christmas Day and Good Friday), and may not be released within that time except on a judge's direction.

In the Magistrates' Domestic Court the remedies available depend on the level of risk. If the respondent has already used or threatened to use violence against the applicant or any child of the family, a domestic court may make an order that the other spouse shall not use or threaten violence or incite anyone else to do so. However, where there is either substantial evidence of the respondent causing physical injury to the applicant or a child of the family or evidence of a threat to do so and actual violence against another person, or the respondent has threatened to use violence in breach of a previous order, the court may exclude a spouse from the matrimonial home or order that the applicant be permitted to return. The order forbids the respondent to use violence or to enter the matrimonial home (1978 Act, s.16).

In addition, if the court is satisfied that the respondent has already physically injured the applicant or a child of the family, and that it is essential for the efficacy of the order, the magistrates may attach a power of arrest to the order. This will have the same effect as under the 1976 Act. If no power of arrest is attached, an applicant may apply for the arrest of a respondent in breach of a personal protection order. The court may then fine up to £1,000 or imprison for not more than 2 months.

3 Housing, education, welfare rights and discrimination

This chapter brings together four areas of the client's life, housing, education, welfare rights and discrimination, in which social workers may be called on to recognize the legal nature of a problem or be helped to give appropriate advice or practical assistance by their understanding of the legal framework.

Housing
Modern housing law is about the right of an occupier not to be unreasonably deprived of his/her home and only to pay a fair rent for it, the efforts of landlords to let out their property at the greatest profit and yet retain the greatest freedom of disposal of it, and the rule of law through the courts which determines the rights and wrongs of a particular situation and interprets the application of statute law to particular arrangements.

Housing law is a vast and complex subject best left to lawyers; however, there are three topics about which social workers need sufficient knowledge to advise their clients:

1. Eviction.
2. Unlawful eviction and harassment.
3. Homeless persons (Housing Act 1985, Part III).

These topics need to be looked at in some detail, after a short introduction on the different possible relationship that may exist between individuals and the 'land' (including any building on that land) that they occupy:

1. They may *own* the land — as freehold owner; or
2. They may have been granted exclusive use of the land for a slice of time in return for payment or services as tenant; or

3. They may have permission to be on the land as the licensee without having a tenancy (as are guests in hotels, residents in hospitals or homes, children in their parents' homes, etc.); or
4. They may be on the land without permission as a trespasser.

The occuper's rights and duties are determined by his/her relationship to the land. In particular, the distinction between a *tenant* and a *licensee* is important because tenants have much statutory protection from eviction and rent increases under the Rent and Housing Acts and licensees have very little, although they may be entitled to protection from immediate eviction. Trespassers have no protection, except for recourse to the courts if undue force is used against them.

It is an overriding principle that it is the law, and not the parties, which determines the form of the relationship. A landlord may not, for instance, evade the consequences of what is effectively a tenancy by describing the tenant as a 'licensee'.

Eviction
If a landlord wishes to regain possession of his property, he can only do so, whether or not the tenancy is at an end, if the tenant agrees (without unlawful pressure, see p. 27) to leave. If the tenant does not agree to leave, and

(a)   the tenant breaks a term of the lease or tenancy agreement;
(b)   the tenant is paying on a weekly or monthly basis and protected by the Rent Acts;
(c)   the tenant is paying on a weekly or monthly basis but is not protected by the Rent Acts

then the landlord must give valid notice to quit and get an eviction order from the County Court. Only then will he be entitled to evict the tenant, with the help of the bailiff if necessary.

It is important for social workers to advise their clients that they should not leave on threat of a court order, and that unless they are agreeable to leaving, any tenant served with a County Court summons for possession should seek immediate legal advice (currently available under the 'green-form' scheme) as to their rights and how to contest the landlord's application. Although they may not be ultimately successful in retaining the accommodation, they may well be able to get an extension of time before the eviction order can be executed. If no application is made to the court on behalf of the tenant, the landlord may, provided the formalities are satisfied, be granted an immediate eviction order.

Unlawful eviction and harassment
People are unlawfully evicted if they are physically evicted from premises they are entitled (see above) to occupy without an eviction order being in force. Harassment consists of making life so unpleasant that the tenant leaves, or stays but fails to complain to the rent officer or public health inspector of the treatment he/she is subjected to. Both unlawful eviction and harassment are actionable as criminal proceedings under the Protection from Eviction Act 1977 or civil proceedings.

The 'Residential Occupier' referred to in the definitions in sections 1(2) and 1(3) of the 1977 Act protects almost anyone living on premises, except certain trespassers or licensees whose licence has ended.

All in all, landlords are well advised always to seek a court order before evicting an occupier, and social workers should act at once to seek legal advice on behalf of a client threatened with eviction who is more likely to be protected as a 'residential occupier' than not.

Criminal proceedings are only rarely brought, usually by the Tenancy Relations or Harassment Officer of the local authority. Where they are brought, the delay is often too great to benefit the evicted person except, possibly, in terms of compensation. Civil proceedings may be brought in the County Court (or High Court if large damages are sought). The injured party may seek an injunction, an order of the court which identifies the person bound by it and makes him liable if he fails to comply with it for contempt of court which can be dealt with by fine or imprisonment.

A full injunction is normally made at the end of lengthy proceedings but in an emergency an occupier who can be shown to have acted without delay may apply with an affidavit to a court or a judge in chambers for an *ex parte* injunction which will last for a few days until a court hearing *inter partes*. At the *inter partes* hearing the court may issue an interim injunction to last until the full hearing.

At the full hearing damages may be awarded. They may be special — to cover actual loss; or general — for shock and injury; or aggravated — when the treatment was particularly brutal or offensive; or exemplary — to teach the landlord a lesson.

In order to help a client to obtain relief, speed and specialist legal advice from a Law Centre or a private practitioner is essential. It is important to make note of any incidents which may amount to harassment for use as evidence.

Homeless persons

The basic aims of the Housing (Homeless Persons) Act 1977, the provisions of which are now consolidated into the Housing Act 1985, Part III, were to impose on local housing authorities a statutory duty to rehouse homeless families, and to provide clear guidelines for determining whether a homeless family falls within the responsibility of one local authority rather than another. The policy of the Act is to keep families together by placing on local housing authorities a duty to provide full and permanent rehousing for those who satisfy the qualifying conditions. A substantial body of case law has grown up around the statutory provisions (Hoath, 1983). In order to qualify for full and permanent rehousing certain criteria have to be satisfied, as follows.

Homelessness which is not intentional The applicant must be homeless and must not be intentionally so. Section 58 of the Housing Act 1985 defines a person as being 'homeless' if he has no accommodation available for occupation by himself together with any member of his family living with him and any other person who normally lives with him 'in circumstances which the housing authority considers it reasonable for that person to do so'. Accommodation is 'available' if there is some place which the claimant is entitled to occupy as owner or tenant, or he has a court order entitling him to occupy. In the same way, an occupier who has a contractual or bare licence or entitlement to occupy because the landlord has not obtained a possession order, and eviction would be unlawful, cannot qualify as homeless under the Act. On the other hand, lack of a place to park a mobile home or moor a houseboat counts as 'homelessness'.

If the authority seeks to avoid responsibility for rehousing on the ground that the applicant is intentionally homeless, the onus of proof is on them. Under section 60 of the 1985 Act, it is stated:

> A person becomes homeless intentionally if he deliberately does or fails to do anything in consequence of which he ceases to occupy accommodation which is available for his occupation and which it would have been reasonable for him to occupy [e.g. fails to pay the rent and is lawfully evicted].

However, if the loss of accommodation arises from genuine ignorance of a legal right to continue occupation, the person should not be treated as being intentionally homeless. This might occur where a tenant, given notice to quit, left premises because he/she was unaware of the right to remain in occupation until the expiry of a court order.

Priority need   The original legislation was designed to protect vulnerable people and to ensure that lack of a home would not result in families being split up. Prior to the 1977 Act, homeless families were often in a catch-22 situation where the children were in care because of lack of accommodation and the parents were not entitled to accommodation because the children were in care. Under the 1985 Act, a person has priority need if:

(a) he has dependent children living with him, or who might reasonably be expected to live with him;
(b) he becomes homeless through flood, fire or other disaster;
(c) he or anyone who lives or might reasonably be expected to live with him is especially vulnerable because of age, disability or other special reasons;
(d) she, or a woman who does or might reasonably be expected to live with the applicant, is pregnant.

Those who have a priority need but may have become intentionally homeless are entitled to temporary accommodation (e.g. bed and breakfast) to give them a chance to make permanent arrangements, and homeless people without a priority need may receive a lesser degree of assistance.

A local connection   Applicants must be accepted by the authority to which they apply 'unless he and anyone who might reasonably be expected to live with him has no connection with that authority and does have a connection with another' (1985 Act, s.61). A person may have a local connection because he either lives, or once lived, in an area, or because he is employed there, or because of family connections, or any special circumstances. Anyone who is homeless as a result of domestic violence does not have to establish a local connection in the area to which he/she applies.

It will be apparent that given the amount of case law that has built up around the provisions specialist legal advice may be essential in complex cases.

In a situation in which there are more homeless people than available housing, many authorities are under intolerable strain. Until 1986 dissatisfied claimants frequently, and often successfully, resorted to judicial review since it provided the only effective appeal against a housing authority's decision in cases under the Act. The decision of the House of Lords in *Puhlhofer* v. *London Borough of Hillingdon* [1986], that judicial review should not be regarded as the normal remedy for the lack of any other right of appeal but should only be available in exceptional cases, has substantially reduced the number of applications (Ball, 1987d).

Education
Local authorities have considerable statutory obligations under the Education Act 1944, as amended by subsequent Education Acts, to provide and maintain an efficient education service and to ensure that parents, guardians and others caring for children meet their obligations in respect of the children's education; the legislation in this field is both detailed and, because of its vulnerability to political whim, prone to frequent change. In terms of their practice, it is suggested that there are two areas of education law with which social workers need to be familiar: the legal

consequences following from parental failure to ensure a child's attendance at school, and the statutory provisions regarding children with special educational needs.

School attendance

The legal duty to ensure attendance rests with parents or guardians or, in practice, anyone else caring for a child *in loco parentes*. Every child must receive full-time education from, at the latest, the term after their fifth birthday until, at the earliest, the end of the Easter term following their sixteenth birthday, if this is before the end of January, or on the Friday before the last Monday in May if the birthday falls between the end of January and 1 September. Under the Education Act 1980, parents may express a preference as to the school they wish their child to attend.

Every local education authority (LEA) has a team of education welfare officers (EWOs) part of whose responsibility is to follow up irregular attendance and to seek to improve it. The nature of the role and the status of EWOs varies markedly in different authorities; in some they perform and are recognized as sophisticated social workers within the educational system, while at the other extreme their role and status have not developed from that of the school attendance officer.

When there is concern about a child's school attendance, and informal efforts to improve it have failed, parents are served with a written notice of the LEA's intention to serve a school attendance order (Education Act 1944, s.37, as amended). The notice must specify the school it is intended to name in the order and may list suitable alternative schools. Parents may at this stage opt for the name of one of these, which will then be named in the order. Once the school attendance order is issued, the child's failure to attend the named school renders the parents liable to proceedings in the Magistrates' Court. Fines may be imposed for the first two offences and prison sentences of up to 1 month subsequently.

Whether or not the parents are proceeded against, the child may be brought before the Juvenile Court in care proceedings under the Children and Young Persons Act 1969, s.1(2)(e), on the grounds that 'he is not receiving full time education suitable to his age, ability and aptitude' and is 'in need of care or control' that he will not receive unless an order is made under the Act. The orders that may be made in care proceedings appear on p. 62.

If parents choose to educate their children at home or to send them to a 'free' school (an independent school not registered as such by the Department of Education and Science), the LEA must satisfy itself that the provision is 'appropriate' and the onus of proof is on the parent. If the authority is not satisfied, it may issue a school attendance order.

Special educational needs

The Education Act 1981   Implemented in 1984, it is the legislative response to the *Report of the Committee of Enquiry into the Education of Handicapped Children and Young People*, chaired by Baroness Warnock (HMSO, 1978).

A child has special educational needs if he/she has a learning difficulty which requires special educational provision. Learning difficulty is defined as:

(a) a significantly greater difficulty in learning than the majority of children of his age;
(b) a disability which prevents him making use of educational facilities of the kind usually provided in school within the LEA for children of his age.

Any child under 5 years who is or would be likely to fall into either of the above categories on reaching school age unless special educational provision were made is defined as having special learning difficulties, although no child may be so regarded solely because the language or form of language used at any time at home is different from that used at school.

Special educational provision is defined as any educational provision for a child under 2 years of age, and that which is additional to, or different from, education provision in schools maintained by the LEA for children over 2 years. Interpretation of 'learning difficulty' is problematic and has resulted in several case decisions (Ball, 1987a; Liell and Saunders, 1987).

When an LEA decides that a child needs assessment as to whether he/she has special educational needs, a notice must be served on the parents or guardian of that decision and the procedure that will be followed (1981 Act, s.5). If following the assessment the LEA decides that no special provision is required, the parents may appeal to the Secretary of State for Education who has the power to direct the authority to reconsider, but he cannot direct them to act differently.

If the authority decides that special provision is required, it has to make a 'Statement' of the child's educational needs and is under a duty to 'arrange that special educational provision specified in the statement is made for him unless his parents make suitable arrangements' (s.7(2)).

The underlying philosophy of the Warnock Report and the basic strategy of the Act is that, wherever possible, special provision should be made within ordinary schools and only where this is not appropriate should children be sent to special schools. Parents wishing to appeal against the provision proposed for their child have to appeal first to an Appeal Committee which may confirm the decision or remit it to the LEA for reconsideration. A parent who is still not satisfied may appeal to the Secretary of State who at this stage has the power – very occasionally used – to direct the authority to make other provision.

Research into the working of the 1981 Act reveals a sad catalogue of long delays, blanket policies and failure to treat individual cases on their merits (Stone, 1987). Social workers have a key role to play in supporting parents in the exercise of the limited rights that they have under the Act. The relative powerlessness of parents in this procedure is underlined by the divisional court's ruling in *R. v. Hereford and Worcester County Council or Another, ex parte Lashford* [1987] that even if an LEA decides that a child has special educational needs, it has also a discretion as to whether or not special provision is required, and if it is decided that it is not, it cannot be compelled to make a Statement under s.7(1).

Welfare rights

The term 'welfare rights' is used here as meaning entitlement to payment of benefit from the state either on the basis of contributions paid or a particular status – childhood, old age or handicap – or entitlement for a variety of reasons to income support.

The legal framework of the provision of benefit is necessary to an understanding of the welfare rights system (however, the detailed working of the system, although an essential part of social work practice, is beyond the scope of an introductory text). Excellent up-to-date, detailed guidance on entitlement and the practicalities of submitting and pursuing claims is published annually by the Child Poverty Action Group (CPAG), the Disability Alliance and other organizations; useful wall-chart guides are also produced by *Community Care* and other social work publications. In order to make any sense of the tangled maze of available benefit, it may be helpful to consider the basic distinction between those benefits to which there is entitlement regardless of means and those which are means-tested. The non-means-tested social security benefits include all those towards which National Insurance Contributions are paid, together with those such as child benefit which are paid as of right without contribution or means-test. National welfare benefits are all income related and therefore means-tested. The two categories will be considered separately.

Non-means-tested social security benefits

National Insurance Contributions   There are four different classes of contributions paid on the basis of an 'earnings factor' by different categories of people between school-leaving and retirement age which give rise to varying entitlement to benefit. A fixed percentage of all contributions goes towards funding the National Health Service and the rest towards national insurance benefits.

Table 1   Classes of National Insurance Contribution

Class	Paid by:	Entitlement
1	Jointly by employed earners and their employers	All contributory benefits
2	Self-employed	All except unemployment
3	Voluntary contributions	Widows benefit and retirement pension
4	Self-employed with profits above prescribed level	None

The principal benefits, excluding retirement and industrial injuries benefit, are:

1. *Unemployment benefit* Payable after 3 days' unemployment to those who satisfy the contributions conditions and sign on as available for work at the unemployment benefit office. Unemployment benefit is paid for a maximum of 312 days, after which there must be a further period of work before it can be reclaimed (for greater detail, see Rowland, 1988, s.2).

2. *Benefits for those incapable of work on medical grounds* Most employees who are away from work due to illness receive statutory sick pay (SSP) from their employers for the first 28 weeks; those who do not and have paid the appropriate contributions will be entitled to sickness benefit. After 28 weeks, there may be entitlement to invalidity benefit or, in certain circumstances, to severe disablement allowance. For all these benefits medical evidence will be required (Rowland, 1988, s.3).

3. *Maternity benefit* Statutory maternity pay (SMP), now the main source of income for pregnant women, is the minimum maternity pay a woman who has worked continuously for the same employer for at least 6 months, and who satisfies the earnings conditions, is entitled to from her employer. Maternity allowance is payable to pregnant women who satisfy the employment requirements but are not entitled to statutory maternity pay.

4. *Widows benefit* Entitlement to benefit depends on the woman's husband's contributions, her age when widowed and whether she has dependent children.

Non-contributory benefits relating to status or disability

Benefits for children Child benefit is payable for all children under school-leaving age, or aged 16–19 and in full-time education. Payment is made to a parent or other who is 'responsible' for the child, either because he/she lives as a child of the family or the parent pays at least the current rate of benefit for maintenance of the child.

The elderly Certain very elderly people who are not entitled to retirement and contribution-related pensions may be entitled to a small pension if they satisfy other conditions (Rowland, 1988, ch.5).

Benefits payable to the severely disabled

(a) *Mobility allowance (Social Security Act 1975, s.37A)* This is designed to help those between the ages of 5 and 65 (continuing to 75 for those already in receipt) who are unable, or virtually unable, to walk and are likely to remain so for at least 12 months. It is not taxable and is disregarded in the assessment of resources for the principal means-tested benefits. Persons provided with an invalid carriage or adapted car are not also entitled to a mobility allowance, though they may transfer to that scheme or use their mobility allowance to buy or hire a car.

(b) *Attendance allowance (Social Security Act 1975, s.35 (1))* A person is entitled to an attendance allowance if he/she satisfies the prescribed conditions as to residence and either

(i) is so severely disabled physically or mentally that, by day, requires from another person:

— frequent attention throughout the day in connection with bodily functions, or

— continual supervision throughout the day in order to avoid substantial danger to self or to others;

(ii) is so severely disabled physically or mentally that, at night, requires from another person:

— prolonged or repeated attention during the night in connection with bodily functions, or

— continual supervision throughout the night in order to avoid substantial danger to self or to others.

Entitlement to an attendance allowance is determined by Adjudication Officers and the Attendance Allowance Board. The allowance may be payable at a higher or lower rate according to whether the disabled person needs the prescribed attention throughout the 24 hours or only by night or only by day. The allowance is not

taxable, and not taken into account when entitlement to supplementary benefit is being assessed.
(c) *Invalid care allowance (Social Security Act 1975, s.37)* Here provision is for an allowance for a claimant who can establish that he is engaged for at least 35 hours per week in caring for a severely disabled person in receipt of an attendance allowance or industrial injuries constant attendance allowance. A carer is not eligible for ICA if earning more than £12 per week from employment or in full-time education.

(For greater detail consult the DHSS Guide HB5 and the Disability Alliance *Disability Rights Handbook*.)

Claims
Apart from unemployment benefit and family credit, all social security benefit claims will usually be dealt with, at least initially, by the DHSS local office, where all inquiries should be made. Entitlement to most benefits depends on a claim being submitted on the appropriate DHSS form, usually provided with the booklet describing the particular benefit. Although a limited amount of backdating is possible, those who may be entitled to benefit should be encouraged to claim at once as there are strict time limits which can only be extended 'for good cause'.

Most initial decisions on claims are taken by the Adjudication Officer, who should reach a decision within 14 days. Undue delay may be grounds for complaint to the Ombudsman. When the Adjudication Officer has reached a decision, a dissatisfied applicant can appeal in writing to a social security appeal tribunal made up of a legally qualified chairperson and two others. The Child Poverty Action Group (CPAG) provide detailed advice on the conduct of appeals (Rowland, 1988).

National welfare income-related benefits
The Social Security Act 1986 introduced major changes in the main income-related benefits and, in particular, to the single payments scheme for exceptional needs now replaced with discretionary payments from the social fund, most in the form of loans. This book can only offer an outline guide to the legal basis of provision; details of entitlement and

procedures for claiming are set out in detail and with great clarity (considering the complexity) in CPAG's annually published *National Welfare Benefits Handbook* (see Lakhani *et al.* 1988).

The three main income-related benefits are Income Support (IS) for those not in full-time work; Family Credit (FC) for those in low-paid employment; and Housing Benefit (HB) to help with the payment of rent and rates.

Income Support is intended to be the safety net of the welfare state. Anyone who has capital of less than £6,000 and is not in full-time work (24 hours or more a week), and whose partner is not in full-time work and whose income drops below the level laid down annually by Parliament, is, provided that certain conditions are satisfied, entitled to have his/her income brought up to the IS level.

The general conditions that have to be satisfied by claimants for IS relate to age, residence and work. Entitlement to IS is calculated on the basis of the applicable amount for the claimant, partner and children according to their age, less any deductions for income or capital (£3,000–£6,000), plus any premiums payable in recognition of age, ill-health or other additional family responsibilities (Lakhani *et al.*, 1988, s.2).

Those in receipt of IS will also be entitled to HB (see below). Claimants living in special sorts of accommodation, such as residential care or board and lodging accommodation, have their IS calculated on the basis of an amount for personal expenses and an allowance towards the costs of accommodation. Claims for IS are made to local DHSS offices, and decisions are reached by adjudication officers and may be appealed against to social security appeal tribunals.

Family Credit replaced Family Income Supplement for families in low-paid work in April 1988. It is paid to couples and single parents with dependent children when the claimant or partner works 24 hours or more each week, meets the residence requirements and has capital of less than £6,000. The amount of FC paid depends on the size of the family, their income and any capital between £3,000 and £6,000 for which deductions are made.

Claims for FC are made to the DHSS on the form accompanying the leaflet FC1 obtaining from those offices, or most post offices. Unlike IS, all claims are processed centrally by the Family Credit Unit at Blackpool, although appeals against miscalculation or refusal of FC lie to a social security appeal tribunal.

Those in receipt of FC are not entitled to IS, but may qualify for HB and, as with those on IS, for help in the future towards payment of the Community Charge. Receipt of IS or FC will, in many circumstances, entitle claimants to additional medical and educational benefits and to legal aid.

Housing Benefit is a national scheme run by local authorities designed to help people on low incomes, whether married or single and with or without children, to pay their rent and rates. The legal framework of the scheme is set out in the Social Security Act 1986, Part II. The very complex law and regulations with an expert commentary can be found in CPAG's *Annotated Housing Benefit Legislation 1988/89* and in publications by housing pressure groups. Housing law is constantly being developed by judicial decision; reports of important cases with commentary are published in *Legal Action*, the monthly bulletin of the Legal Action Group.

Claims for HB have to be made in writing to the local authority, unless the claimant is already claiming IS, in which case claims may be directed either to the authority or the DHSS who forward them. Although the law is complex, the basic principles of HB calculations are simple; their application is again made clear by CPAG's step-by-step guide (Lakhani *et al.*, 1988, s.4.5).

The local authority should reach a decision on HB within 14 days of receiving a valid claim and must notify the applicant in writing. Dissatisfied applicants may ask for a more detailed explanation and an internal review by an HB officer on the basis of written comments on the decision. Beyond this, there is no independent appeal tribunal, although the applicant may put his case to a review board made up of three local councillors.

The Social Fund
Death and maternity grants paid regardless of income and additional payments of supplementary benefit for special expenses were abolished by the 1986 Act and replaced with grants from the Social Fund payable on a non-discretionary

basis for funeral, maternity and severe weather payments (hopefully), and on a highly controversial discretionary basis for exceptional needs payments.

Payments from the non-discretionary Social Fund depend on eligibility through current entitlement to IS, FC or HB. The cash-limited Social Fund provides for budgeting loans which are repayable, and community care grants which are not. Budgeting loans may be made to claimants on IS for a variety of immediate needs. Community care grants are intended to help with the re-establishment of those leaving residential care or to help prevent the need for a move into care. The experience of those who have assisted claimants suggests that considerable help with form-filling and perseverance in pursuing claims is necessary. Claims for loans or grants have to be made to Social Fund Officers (SFOs) in DHSS offices, who reach their decisions on the basis of the law, 'directions' issued by the Secretary of State which must be followed and 'guidance' which SFOs must take account of. Extracts from this 'guidance' are included in CPAG's *National Welfare Benefits Handbook* (Lakhani *et al.*, 1988). A dissatisfied claimant has the right to ask for review by the SFO who made the decision, and if still dissatisfied, to a further review by a Social Fund Inspector. There is no right of appeal to a tribunal.

Discrimination
Discrimination exists in many forms. It is legislated against only in the areas of race and sex, and the effectiveness of existing legislation is frequently called into question. The Race Relations Act 1976, and the Sexual Discrimination Act 1975, make very similar provision by making overtly discriminatory behaviour a criminal offence and by setting up the Commission for Racial Equality and Equal Opportunities Commission to monitor the legislation and encourage good practice. Legislation in this field is a blunt instrument, the limitation of which is manifestly apparent. (Detailed examination of the legislation and its application to particular situations is beyond the scope of this book and reference should be made to specialist texts, Lustgarten, 1980; Pannick, 1985.)

4 The criminal process

The police and their powers

The Police and Criminal Evidence Act 1984 provides a statutory framework within which the police must operate when investigating crime; most of the Act was implemented in January 1986. It replaces provisions in several statutes, and most important, the 'Judges' Rules', a series of administrative directions which previously regulated police interviews and the evidence obtained from interrogation. The Act finally reached the statute-book after several years of official inquiries, evidence taken from interested parties, two Bills and the longest — and one of the most acrimonious — Parliamentary debates over major legislation in recent years. Experience of Police and Criminal Evidence Act 1984 (PACE) procedures is resulting in a continuing police and civil liberties debate, especially over the right to silence.

The law is contained in the Act, supported by four critically important Codes of Practice, which while they are not law, have a higher status than the 'Judges' Rules', in that although a breach of the Codes cannot itself be made the subject of criminal proceedings or the foundation of a civil action for damages, any breach is an automatic breach of police discipline and therefore may be the subject of disciplinary proceedings.

The Codes of Practice provide an elaborate system of rules for dealing with suspects:

1. In a police station.
2. In relation to 'stop and search'.
3. In relation to search of premises.
4. In an identification situation.

In a trial the defence will be able to refer to a breach of the

Code, but evidence obtained in breach will not automatically be excluded, although a recent Court of Appeal decision shows that its admission may be grounds for appeal if a 'guilty' verdict was rendered unsafe (*R.* v. *Delany* [1988]). The test in relation to confessions — the most critical area — has been considerably altered by section 76 of the Act. The old test of the confession only being admissible if it was not obtained 'by oppression' and if 'voluntary' has been altered. The 1984 Act retains the exclusion of evidence obtained by 'oppression' which is defined, but it replaces the old test of whether the confession had been obtained by 'fear of prejudice or hope of advantage' with one which questions whether anything said or done at the time at which the confession was made was likely 'in the circumstances existing at the time, to render unreliable any confession which might be made . . . in consequence thereof' (*R.* v. *Delany* [1988]). As a measure of protection for the defendant, the statute firmly puts the burden of proof that the confession is not 'unreliable' on the prosecution.

The Act also introduced considerable changes in relation to the evidence that spouses may, or may be compelled, to give evidence for or against each other (Zander, 1986). Under the provisions of section 80, spouses are competent and compellable witnesses for the accused unless they are jointly charged. They are competent witnesses for the prosecution in all cases and may be compelled if the case involves violence against the other spouse or against anyone who was under 16 years at the time of the offence, or where the offence was a sexual one against anyone under 16 years (s.80(3)).

'Stop and search'
Under section 1 of the Act, police officers are given the power to search any 'person or vehicle' and 'anything which is in or on a vehicle, for stolen or prohibited articles' and to detain a person or vehicle for the purpose of such a search, provided that there are 'reasonable grounds' for suspecting that stolen or prohibited articles will be found. These include offensive weapons or articles made or adapted for use in burglary, theft, taking a motor vehicle or obtaining property by deception.

The Code defines both 'suspicion' and 'reasonable grounds' restrictively: 'Reasonable suspicion, in contrast to mere suspicion, must be founded on fact. There must be some concrete basis for the officer's belief, related to the person concerned, which can be considered and evaluated by an objective third person.' The degree or level of suspicion required to establish the reasonable grounds justifying the exercise of powers of stop and search is 'no less than the degree or level of suspicion required to effect an arrest' (Code of Practice, Annexe B, para. 1).

The power to stop and search can be exercised in any place to which the public, or a section of the public, have access but not when people or their cars are on their own private land, or on private land on which they have specific permission to be. Searches on those premises require a search warrant.

The Act (s.2) lays down procedural safeguards to prevent abuse of the power to stop and search. These involve the police having to identify themselves and provide the owner of a vehicle with a written record of the search. The person searched must be detained for no longer than the search takes.

Powers of entry, search and seizure
Warrants to *enter and search premises* for evidence of serious arrestable offences are issued on application to a Justice of the Peace. The application must give reasonable grounds for believing that the offence has been committed, and there is material on the premises likely to be of value and relevant to the investigation, which is not 'excluded', or 'special' procedure material, and that access to the premises is impracticable without a warrant. Warrants to search for records held on confidential files, medical samples and some journalistic material can only be granted by circuit judges (Police and Criminal Evidence Act 1984, s.9).

Arrest
Arrest may be lawfully effected in a number of ways, depending on the seriousness of the offences.

Arrest by the police without a warrant
Where a constable has reasonable grounds for suspecting that an arrestable offence has been committed, he may arrest without warrant

1. anyone whom he has reasonable grounds for suspecting to be guilty of an offence;
2. anyone who is about to commit; or
3. anyone whom he has reasonable grounds to suspect to be about to commit an arrestable offence (s.24);
4. anyone who has within the previous month been convicted of a recordable offence, for which he was not held in police custody, for the purpose of taking his fingerprints if he has failed to comply within 7 days to a request to attend a police station for this purpose (s.27).

The power of arrest for arrestable offences applies

1. to offences for which the penalty is fixed by law (e.g. murder and treason);
2. to offences carrying a penalty of 5 or more years' imprisonment;
3. to offences in subsection 2 — some fairly serious offences which were not previously arrestable.

General arrest conditions (s.25)   All other offences carry a limited power of arrest if a constable has reasonable grounds for suspecting that any offence has been committed or attempted, or is being committed or attempted, and it appears to him that service of a summons is impracticable or inappropriate because any of the 'general arrest conditions' is satisfied. These are that:

(a) The officer does not know and cannot readily obtain the name and address of the suspect, or he reasonably believes them to be false, or he doubts whether the suspect has given an adequate address for service of a summons.
(b) There are reasonable grounds for believing that the arrest is necessary to prevent the suspect causing:
    — physical harm to himself or to someone else;
    — loss of or damage to property;
    — an unlawful obstruction of the highway;
    — an offence against public decency where the public cannot easily avoid the person to be arrested;
    — to protect the child 'or other vulnerable person from the person to be arrested'.

An arrested person must be told at once, or as soon as is practicable, that he is under arrest and the grounds — even if these may be obvious.

Arrest under warrant An arrest warrant may be issued by a Justice of the Peace for a serious offence where the offender is unlikely to, or has failed to answer, a summons.

Citizen's arrest Any person has a right to arrest without warrant anyone who is committing, or is reasonably suspected of having committed, an offence. This right has not been affected by the Act.

Detention

Where a person attends voluntarily at a police station to assist with an investigation 'he shall be entitled to leave at will unless he is placed under arrest' (s.29), and where a person is arrested anywhere other than in a police station, the Act provides that he should be taken to a police station 'as soon as is practicable'. If there is a delay, the reasons for this must be recorded. Previously detention in a police station and interrogation by the police was regulated by the 'Judges' Rules'; since the implementation of Part IV of the 1984 Act, these have been replaced by the new statutory framework supported by a separate Code of Practice. Detention in a police station must be in conformity with the provisions of the Act and the custody officer, who will usually be of the rank of sergeant or above and should not be involved in the investigation, and who must order the release of anyone whose continued detention by the police cannot be justified under the Act.

Rights of an arrested person to information

As soon as practicable after arrival at the police station or after his arrest there, an arrested person must be told

1. of the grounds of his detention;
2. of the right to have someone informed;
3. of the right to consult a copy of the Codes;
4. of the right to legal advice.

Duties of the custody officer

The Act lays down that it is the duty of the custody officer to ensure that a person brought to a police station is charged if there is enough evidence to charge him, or released if there is not, unless there are reasonable grounds for believing that his detention is needed to preserve or obtain evidence of the offence for which he was arrested (s.37). As soon as is practicable, the custody officer must make a written record of the grounds of detention, preferably in the presence of the suspect who must be told of the grounds. The need for further detention must be reviewed by a review officer, of at least the rank of inspector, who has not been involved in the investigation, after 6 hours and thereafter at 9-hourly intervals. If the police wish to hold the suspect without putting charges after 24 hours, authorization must be given by a superintendent, or officer above, after hearing representations from the suspect or his solicitor, and after 36 hours approval must be obtained from a Magistrates' Court. The court can approve a further 36 hours (twice) up to an absolute maximum of 96 hours. There is limited provision in the Act for flexible interpretation of the time limits.

Questioning and treatment of persons by the police

The Custody Officer must take charge of searches of detained persons and make an inventory of the suspect's property. There may only be a search if the officer considers it necessary to make a complete list of his property, and a suspect may only be searched by a constable of the same sex. If a strip search is considered necessary, the reason must be recorded.

Intimate searches are allowed only if authorized by a superintendent or above, on the grounds of reasonable belief that the arrested person might have concealed anything that could be used to cause injury to himself or others, and that he might so use it, and that it could only be discovered by such a search.

When a person is under arrest in a police station, he is entitled, if he so requests, 'to have one friend or relative or other person who is known to him and likely to take an interest in his welfare' told as soon as is practicable that he is under arrest and his whereabouts (s.56). If the arrested person is a juvenile, the parents must be informed as well as any agency to whom they are under supervision or a care order. Delay is only permissible in the case of serious arrestable offences. The Act provides that a person held in custody is 'entitled, if he so requests, to consult a solicitor privately at any time' — with the same proviso for serious arrestable offences. The 24-hour duty solicitor scheme should ensure that a solicitor can always be contacted (Ball, 1986a).

The Code of Practice on Detention, Treatment and Questioning (para. 10) replaces the 'Judges' Rules' provisions in relation to cautions. Rule 10 provides that a person whom there are grounds for suspecting of an offence must be cautioned before any questions, or further questions, are put to him for the purpose of obtaining evidence which may be given to a court in a prosecution. The caution must be in the following terms: 'You do not have to say anything unless you wish to do so, but what you say may be given in evidence.'

When a detained person has been charged or a person has been informed that he may be prosecuted for an offence, he should be cautioned again. A charged person should be given written details of the offence, the police officer's name and the police station. After the charge is made, questions relating to the offence may not be put, with the exception of those necessary to minimize harm to others or to clear up an ambiguity. Before any such questions, the caution should be administered again.

Under Appendix D of the Code of Practice on Detention, Treatment and Questioning, there are detailed requirements relating to written records of interviews (*R. v. Delany* [1988]). Tape recording of interviews will become the subject of a special Code of Practice and will be introduced at a later date.

Fingerprints should only be taken with consent, but may be taken without consent if a superintendent, or officer above, authorizes it on the grounds of reasonable suspicion of the involvement of that person in an offence and that his fingerprints will tend to confirm or disprove his involvement. In the case of juveniles under 17 years, a parent must consent for a child under 14, and both the parent and the young person where they are aged 14–16. A social worker representing the local authority can give consent for a child in care (Home Office, 1985).

Bail

A person is bailed when he is released from custody to attend at court or at a police station at a specific time. The primary purpose of bail is to secure the attendance of the defendant at court. Failure to attend constitutes a further offence (Bail Act 1976, s.6(1)).

If the police charge a detained person, they must release him on bail unless his name and address cannot be ascertained or are believed on reasonable grounds to be false. They may also detain in custody to appear in court within 36 hours those whom they believe likely to harm others or themselves, or need protection, as well as those they consider unlikely to answer bail or likely to interfere with witnesses or police investigations (Zander, 1985).

When a defendant appears in court following arrest, or when a serious case is unfinished, the court has to decide whether to remand the defendant in custody or release him on bail. The provisions of the Bail Act 1976, which were intended to avoid unnecessary remands in custody, have been criticized both for failing to achieve that and, at the other end of the spectrum, for allowing the release on bail of serious offenders who commit further grave offences. These are currently under review. The presumption under the Act is that bail will be granted unless there are substantial grounds, which must be entered on the court record, for believing that the defendant if released would fail to surrender, commit further offences, interfere with witnesses or otherwise obstruct the course of justice. All the evidence suggests that there is a very wide discrepancy in the way that courts interpret these provisions (Bottomley, 1973). Bail may be granted unconditionally or subject to conditions imposed to ensure that any of the above grounds which might justify custody are avoided.

Trial venue

All criminal proceedings begin in the Magistrates' Court and over 90 per cent are concluded there. Magistrates have sole jurisdiction over all summary offences, but none over the most serious offences which are triable only on indictment; they may hear the substantial range of cases that can be tried 'either way' (Criminal Law Act 1977, s.19). If the case is triable on an indictment or is triable either way and the defendant elects jury trial, or the magistrates decide that their maximum sentence of £2,000 and/or 6 months' imprisonment would not be adequate, the defendant will be committed for trial either on bail or remanded in custody. Detailed accounts of the criminal trial, the process of sentencing and of the range of sentences available to the magistrates and the Crown Court are major topics well covered elsewhere (Barnard, 1988; Stone, 1988; Walker, 1985).

PART II
THE LEGAL CONTEXT OF
CHILD CARE PRACTICE

Introduction

Local authorities have wide statutory powers and duties to investigate and act to protect children and make caring provision for them. These powers include preventative work and voluntary arrangements, as well as compulsory intervention. The duties include the provision of supervision in the community, short- and long-term care and, in some cases, the placing of children with new families for adoption.

Child care law is that part of the law which concerns the state's duty to protect and provide for children who have no parents or guardians, or whose parents or guardians are unable or unwilling to provide a home for them or adequate care or control within that home. At the present time, both the substantive law which is unduly complex, and the courts within which it is administered, which have inappropriate and overlapping jurisdictions, are long overdue for reform. It seems likely that some measure of reform, at least of the substantive law, will be achieved within the life of the current Parliament, and indication will be given in the text of likely changes where these are already known.

Even more than with some of the other areas of the law in which social workers need to be professionally competent, child care law requires reference to specialist texts. What is provided here cannot be more than a preliminary introduction to a most complex subject, together with some indication of proposed changes in the law and references for further reading.

Currently there are almost twenty routes into care if all emergency, remand and other short-term provisions are included; however, the most commonly used are contained in two (considerably amended) statutes, namely the Child Care Act 1980 and the Children and Young Persons Act 1969.

The 1980 Act, a consolidating statute, with its historical origins in the responsibility of Poor Law authorities to care for destitute and abandoned children, brings together provisions for local authorities to spend money to prevent the need for children to come into care (s.1), to receive children voluntarily into care when their families are unable to provide for them in the short- or long-term (s.2), together with all the powers and duties of local authorities in regard to children in care (Part III). Since its implementation, major amendments to this Act have been introduced by subsequent legislation; these include the provisions regarding parental access to children in care (s.12(A)–(F)), introduced by the Health and Social Services and Social Security Adjudications Act 1983 (s.6, Schedule 1), and those restricting local authorities' powers to detain children in care in secure accommodation without sanction from a court (s.21(A)), introduced under s.9, Schedule 2, of the same Act.

The 1969 Act was intended as a major piece of reforming legislation, which had it been fully implemented, would have decriminalized proceedings against juvenile offenders (Bottoms, 1974); it contains most of the major provisions for protecting neglected, ill-treated, troublesome or delinquent children both in an emergency and through court proceedings. This Act has been considerably altered by subsequent legislation since its partial implementation in 1971, and it has been further amended by the provisions of the Children and Young Persons (Amendment) Act 1986.

Reform of child care law
Throughout the past decade the expressions of dissatisfaction with the current state of the law in this area are typified by Lord Ormrod describing it to a BAAF Conference, in 1982, as being 'in a state of confusion which is unparalleled in any other branch of the law now or at any other time'; and by a High Court judge's description of 'a legislative thicket through which even the most practised members of the legal and social work professions have to struggle' (*R.* v. *Corby Juvenile Court, ex parte M.* [1987], *per* Waite, J.).

The extent of public concern over the state of child care law, and of its negative impact on those caught up in the process, first reached a wider audience through the report of the Social Services Committee which made public, in terms which the government could not ignore, the concerns expressed to it by witnesses representing the whole spectrum of child-involved client groups and professional opinion (HMSO, 1984); practitioners giving evidence to the Committee commented that: 'The present state of children's legislation can only be described as complex, confusing and unsatisfactory. The effect and implications of this on children is diverse with far-reaching consequences.'

In an uncharacteristically swift response the DHSS set up an inter-departmental Working Party, with Law Commission support, to review the whole of public child care law (the private law relating to children was already the subject of Law Commission investigation). This group, working to a tight timetable, produced twelve detailed Working Papers setting out the current law, the legal and procedural problems associated with it and the implications of possible reforms. These were circulated for suggestion and comment to agencies and individuals. The Working Party, having considered the response, published its findings and recommendations for public consumption and comment in the *Child Care Law Review* (CCLR, 1985).

In January 1987 the government published its White Paper, *The Law on Child Care and Family Services*, which sets out fairly detailed proposals for the reform of such major aspects as voluntary and respite care, the protection of children in an emergency, the grounds for and nature of care proceedings, requirements on parents whose children are the subject of supervision orders and parental access to children in care (DHSS, 1987).

These official responses have been given an added urgency by the conclusions about the state of child care law (and social workers' ignorance of it) and, in particular, the unsatisfactory nature of place of safety orders in the reports of the Committees of Inquiry into the deaths of Jasmine Beckford (Blom-Cooper, 1985) and Kimberley Carlile (Blom-Cooper, 1987), and the report of the Cleveland Inquiry (Butler-Sloss, 1988).

5 Routes into care and emergency procedures

There are many statutory routes whereby a child may enter care, and although the total number has dropped considerably over the past ten years, there were still some 72,800 in the care of local authorities in England and Wales on 31 March 1985.

Table 2   Children in care on 31 March 1985,
by legal route into care

Legal route	Thousands in care, 31 March 1985	% (approx.)
Child Care Act 1980, s.2	31.3	43
Interim care order or remand	2.2	3
Care order under Children and Young Persons Act 1969	31.5	43.3
Other court orders	7.7	10.6
Total	72.7	100

The majority of children in care are admitted, on a voluntary basis, under section 2 of the Child Care Act 1980, which may (unusually) be followed by an assumption of parental rights by the local authority (s.3). All the other routes into care require a court order. The child may be made the subject of a care order in the Juvenile Court in care or criminal proceedings under the Children and Young Persons Act 1969, or orders in 'exceptional circumstances' committing the child to the care of the local authority in wardship, matrimonial, guardianship, adoption or custodianship proceedings. Each of the routes into care will be considered in this chapter which concludes with the powers authorizing intervention to protect children in an emergency.

Voluntary admission to care

The Child Care Act 1980 (s.2), which empowers local authorities to receive children under 17 years into their care on a voluntary basis, is drafted in such a way as to cover every conceivable situation in which it might be necessary in the interests of a child's welfare for that child to come into care, either with the or in the absence of the agreement of a parent or guardian. On 31 March 1985, 43 per cent of all children in care had been admitted under this section (see Table 2).

The statutory requirement on the local authority under the 1980 Act is that:

> Where it appears to a local authority with respect to a child in their area appearing to them to be under the age of seventeen:
>
> (a) that he has neither parent or guardian or has been and remains abandoned by his parent or guardian or is lost; or
>
> (b) that his parent or guardian are, for the time being or permanently prevented by reason of mental or bodily disease or infirmity or other incapacity or any other circumstances from providing for his proper accommodation, maintenance and upbringing; and
>
> in either case, that the intervention of the local authority under this section is necessary in the interests of the welfare of the child, it shall be the duty of the local authority to receive the child into their care under this section. (s.2(1))

If a child has come into care under this section, the local authority has a duty to keep him/her in care 'so long as the welfare of the child appears to them to require it' up to the age of 18 years (s.2(2)). However, if a parent or guardian wishes to take over the care of the child, he/she must be returned, or where it appears consistent with the welfare of the child, the local authority must try to ensure that this happens or that a relative or friend takes over care of the child. There are many complex issues surrounding voluntary care which are addressed in detail elsewhere and are the subject of proposed changes in the law (Hoggett, 1987, ch. 9; CCLR, 1985; DHSS, 1987).

At the present time, if a child has been in the care of a local authority for more than 6 months, any parent or guardian seeking return of the child to them must give 28 days' notice to the local authority (1980 Act, s.13(2)). This provision was included in the 1975 Children Act in order to encourage a planned return home for children who may have settled into foster homes during their stay in care under section 2, for instance. The proposal in the White Paper to remove this requirement in order to emphasize the voluntary nature of care under this section is not universally welcomed by practitioners.

Under section 1 of the 1980 Act, it is the duty of every local authority to:

> make available such advice, guidance and assistance as may promote the welfare of children by diminishing the need to receive children into or keep them in care . . . or to bring children before a juvenile court.

Different authorities' interpretation of their duties under this section vary widely, both in financial and policy terms, with some authorities making many resources available for preventative work and others limited by a restricted budget; a substantial number of authorities also appear to use the wording of the provision to justify child care policies which favour using compulsory rather than voluntary admission to care (Packman *et al.*, 1986; Vernon and Fruin, 1986; Millham *et al.*, 1986). On the basis of research evidence, and again to emphasize the 'shared' nature of voluntary care, the government proposes that local authorities should no longer be under an obligation to diminish the need to receive children into care, though the duty to avoid doing so compulsorily will remain (DHSS, 1987).

Parental rights resolutions
Under section 3 of the Child Care Act 1980, if grounds as set out in the section exist, local authorities may assume parental rights over children already in their care under section 2. This procedure enables local authorities who believe that it is not in the interests of a child in voluntary care to return home to change the child's care status from voluntary to compulsory by means of a resolution passed

by the social services committee or a designated sub-committee. A resolution may be passed at any time the child is in care under section 2, even though notice has been served by the parents of their intention to remove the child from care (*Lewisham London Borough Council v. Lewisham Juvenile Court Justices* [1980]).

The grounds on which the resolution may be passed are:

(a) that his parents are dead and he has no guardian or custodian; or
(b) that a parent of his
    (i)   has abandoned him, or
    (ii) suffers from some permanent disability rendering him incapable of caring for the child, or
    (iii) while not falling within sub-paragraph (ii) of this paragraph, suffers from a mental disorder (within the meaning of the Mental Health Act 1983), which renders him unfit to care for the child, or
    (iv) is of such habits and mode of life as to be unfit to have the care of the child, or
    (v)   has so consistently failed without reasonable cause to discharge the obligations of a parent as to be unfit to have the care of the child; or
(c) that a resolution under paragraph (b) of this sub-section is in force in relation to one parent of the child who is, or is likely to become a member of the household comprising the child and his other parent; or
(d) that throughout the three years preceding the passing of the resolution the child has been in the care of the local authority under s.2 of this Act, or partly in the care of the local authority and partly in the care of a voluntary organisation.

The local authority may resolve that there shall vest in them the parental rights and duties.

Once the resolution has been passed, any parent or guardian whose rights have been assumed must be contacted and given notice of the resolution and of the right to object. If the parent within 1 month serves notice on the local authority of the objection, the resolution will lapse after 14 days unless the local authority complains to the Juvenile Court. If this is done, the resolution continues in force until the Juvenile Court determines whether it is to continue or lapse.

In these proceedings the parents and the local authority are the parties; if the court decides it is necessary, it may join the child as a party and appoint a guardian ad litem to safe-guard his/her welfare. In order to establish its case, the local authority must satisfy the court that:

1. grounds under s.3(1) existed when the resolution was passed;
2. that grounds (though not necessarily the same ones) still exist (*W*. v. *Nottinghamshire County Council* [1982]);
3. that it is in the interests of the welfare of the child that the resolution should continue.

At the conclusion of the case, the only order the court can make is to confirm the resolution or allow it to lapse. If the resolution is confirmed, or if it was never contested, although the child technically remains in care under section 2 for all practical purposes while the resolution continues, the effect is the same as if the child was the subject of a care order. A parental rights resolution terminates when the child reaches 18 years or is adopted, freed for adoption, made the subject of a custodianship order or a guardian is appointed under the Guardianship of Minors Act 1971 (s.5). The authority may itself rescind the resolution at any time and a parent may apply to the Juvenile Court for the resolution to be ended on the grounds that there were no grounds for making it, or that it is in the child's interests that it should be rescinded.

In response to much adverse comment about practice in regard to the use of section 3, and on the extent to which the power of local authorities to assume parental rights without a court decision is incompatible with the concept of their acting partnership with parents when a child is in voluntary care, the government proposes to abolish the power and to alter the grounds, so that children already in voluntary care are not, should the need arise to prevent their return home, excluded from care proceedings as they are at present (Adcock, White and Rowland, 1983; DHSS, 1987).

Care proceedings
Families whose children are perceived to be in need of local authority care or supervision may not be prepared to accept help on a voluntary basis, or the local authority may not be prepared to offer support without the control of a care order (Packman *et al.*, 1986; Vernon and Fruin, 1986). If this is

the case, proceedings will have to be instituted under the Children and Young Persons Act 1969, s.1; local authorities are bound under section 2 of the Act to investigate any information they receive, suggesting that there are grounds for bringing care proceedings, and to bring the matter to court, unless they are satisfied it is not necessary to do so.

The quasi-criminal nature of care proceedings is reflected in the extent to which the grounds include children who are seen as 'villains' as well as the 'victims' of neglect and child abuse (Packman *et al.*, 1986). This duality leads to a whole series of anomalies which are addressed in the *Child Care Law Review* (CCLR, 1985) and the White Paper (DHSS, 1987).

The grounds on which care proceedings may be brought against a child, aged under 17 years, are set out in s.1(2) of the 1969 Act:

(a) that his proper development is being avoidably prevented or neglected or his health is being avoidably impaired or neglected or he is being ill-treated; or

(b) it is probable that the condition set out in the preceding paragraph will be satisfied in his case having regard to the fact that the court or another court found that the condition was or is satisfied in the case of another child or young person who is or was a member of the household to which he belongs; or

(bb) it is probable that the conditions set out in paragraph (a) of this sub-section will be satisfied in his case, having regard to the fact that a person who has been convicted of an offence mentioned in Schedule I to the Act of 1933 is, or may become, a member of the same household as the child; or

(c) he is exposed to moral danger; or

(d) he is beyond the control of his parents or guardian; or

(e) he is of compulsory school age within the meaning of the Education Act 1944 and is not receiving full-time education suitable to his age, ability and aptitude; or

(f) he is guilty of an offence, excluding homicide.

And also that he is in need of care or control which he is unlikely to receive unless the court makes an order under this section in respect of him.

The proceedings are in two parts: in the first part both the primary grounds under subsections (a)–(f) and the need for care or control have to be established. Only after the grounds have been proved can the court go on to make an order – a further analogy with criminal proceedings where there has to be a finding or admission of guilt before the court can proceed to sentence.

The parties to care proceedings are the local authority or, unusually, the police or National Society for the Protection of Cruelty to Children (NSPCC), as prosecutor, and the child as defendant. Only since the implementation of section 2 of the Children and Young Persons (Amendment) Act 1986, on 1 August 1988, have parents, against whom in neglect and abuse cases the allegations are almost always being made, been able to be joined as parties, although they have for some time been able to receive legal aid to meet any allegations made against them if the court orders that they be represented separately from the child. The court may and according to the dictum in *R. v. Plymouth Juvenile Court, ex parte F.* [1987] should, appoint a guardian ad litem (GAL) to safeguard the welfare of the child in all cases in which separate representation is ordered. Research evidence suggests that rates of appointment of GALs in care proceedings are subject to as wide variations as exist in all other aspects of the juvenile justice system (Murch, 1984; Masson and Shaw, 1988).

If the grounds are proved, the court will then consider all necessary background information to enable it to deal with the case in the child's best interests. At this stage, the justices must consider any reports prepared by the local authority on the child's home circumstances, school record or health, and the GAL's report if there is one. In the future all such reports will be subject to the new disclosure rules referred to in relation to criminal proceedings in the Juvenile Court (see Chapter 9). The court must then decide which of the very limited range of orders to make:

(a) an order requiring the parent or guardian to enter into a recognisance to take proper care or exercise proper control of the child; or

(b) a supervision order, for up to three years (s.11), possibly with a condition of residence with a named individual (s.12(1)) or intermediate treatment under s.12(2); or

(c) a care order committing him to the care of the local authority until his 18th birthday (or 19th if the order was made when he was 16); or

(d) a hospital order within the meaning of the Mental Health Act 1983; or
(e) a guardianship order within the meaning of that Act; or, exceptionally, no order.

The limited right of local authorities and parents to appeal against either the findings in regard to the grounds or the making an order underline the bizarre quasi-criminal nature of the proceedings, as does the fact that the appeal is heard by way of a rehearing in that least suitable forum for family matters, the Crown Court.

On analogy with criminal proceedings, the local authority as 'prosecutor' cannot appeal against the court's decision either to fail to find the grounds proved or to make the order requested or discharge an existing order. They can appeal, by way of case stated, on a point of law only to the Divisional Court of the Family Division. Since the implementation of section 2 of the 1986 Act, parents whose rights may have been profoundly affected by the outcome of the proceedings have a right of appeal on their own behalf, and may only appeal on behalf of their child if there is no GAL; local authorities may resort to the wardship jurisdiction in these circumstances but parents are powerless to do so (see Chapter 7). One of the duties of the GAL is to decide whether to appeal on behalf of the child (DHSS, 1984), and grandparents who may also have been joined as parties to the care proceedings under the 1986 Act may apply to be joined as parties to an appeal although they may not initiate one.

The reform of care proceedings proposed in the White Paper (DHSS, 1987) will remedy many of the more extreme faults that currently exist. The proceedings will be based on a single ground comprising three parts:

1. evidence of harm or likely harm to the child;
2. the absence of a reasonable standard of parental care;
3. the order proposed being the most effective way to safeguard the child's welfare.

Care proceedings based on failure to attend school will be replaced with a currently somewhat vaguely defined education supervision order.

In line with the aim of making family care proceedings less

like criminal proceedings and more like other civil actions involving children, it is proposed that courts ought to be able to make, in addition to the existing range of orders, custody orders in favour of third parties such as grand-parents (CCLR, 1985; DHSS, 1987). In order to reduce the need for full care orders, a new supervision order placing requirements on parents or guardians, rather than on the child as at present, is also proposed. In addition, all parties will have a right of appeal to the Family Division of the High Court.

The protection of children in an emergency
Contrary to widely held beliefs among the general public and despite the local authority's duty to investigate any suspected cases of child abuse or neglect, local authority social workers have no greater powers than any other members of the community to enter property without the consent of the occupier, or to remove children from unsuitable or dangerous surroundings without a warrant. In order to detain children in a place of safety, a social worker — or anyone else — requires an order from a Justice of the Peace. The only exception to this general rule is that social workers have powers of entry, but not by force, and removal, to enable them to carry out their statutory responsibilities in respect of foster children and those placed for adoption (see Chapter 7).

Warrant under the Children and
Young Persons Act 1933 (s.40)
Any person who is acting in the interests of a child can apply, on oath, to a single Justice of the Peace at any time for a warrant on the grounds that:

there is reasonable cause to suspect —

(a) that the child or young person has been or is being assaulted, ill-treated, or neglected in any place within the jurisdiction of the justice, in a manner likely to cause him unnecessary suffering, or injury to health; or
(b) that any offence mentioned in the First Schedule to this Act has been or is being committed in respect of the child or young person.

(The Schedule 1 offences include all offences of causing death or serious injury to a child or young person and attempts to commit the more serious offences.)

The warrant authorizes a named constable to 'search for the child or young person, and, if it is found that he has been or is being assaulted, ill-treated or neglected' to take him to a place of safety (s.40(1)). The person who makes the application may accompany the constable unless the justice directs to the contrary, and the warrant may direct that registered medical practitioner be present when the warrant is executed.

The power, or the threat of it, can be useful in cases where there is a real concern about a child, to whom access is denied, but no actual evidence on which to ground an application for a place of safety order, a situation tragically illustrated by the case of Kimberley Carlile in which, had the social workers or their legal advisers been aware of their powers under s.40, the outcome might have been different (Blom-Cooper, 1987). Although the power, which involves using the police, is an intrusive one, there is an inbuilt safeguard against abuse, in that the power to remove the child is dependent on a finding that the child actually has been 'assaulted, ill-treated, or neglected'. If removal to a place of safety is effected, the order runs for 28 days or any shorter period specified. Unlike a place of safety order under the 1969 Act, time does not begin to run until the warrant is executed.

Place of safety order, Children and Young Persons Act 1969 (s.28(1))

Any person, most usually a social worker, may apply to a single justice at any time on the grounds that they have reasonable cause to believe that:

(a) any of the conditions set out in section 1(2)(a) to (e) of this Act is satisfied in respect of the child or young person; or

(b) an appropriate court would find the condition set out in section 1(2)(b) of this Act satisfied in respect of him; or

(c) the child or young person is about to leave the United Kingdom in contravention of section 25 of the Act of 1933 (which regulates the sending abroad of juvenile entertainers).

The parents and the child need not know of the application, nor need the evidence be given on oath, though many justices will require that it should be. If satisfied, the justice may make an order giving the applicant authority to detain the child and take him/her to a place of safety for a period of up to 28 days or any lesser number. A place of safety is defined in such a way as not to exclude any suitable accommodation:

> a community home provided by a local authority or a controlled community home, any police station or any hospital, surgery, or any other suitable place, the occupier of which is willing temporarily to receive a child or young person. (1933 Act, s.107)

Although the Act speaks of detaining and removing children to a place of safety, applications may be (and frequently are) made in respect of children already in hospital to ensure that they are not removed from a safe place.

It has been recognized for some time, certainly well before events in Cleveland in 1987, that the present powers of social workers to protect children in an emergency are at the same time inadequate in some respects, and overly draconian in others; it is the place of safety order that attracts most criticism in this respect (Ball, 1986b). While there is clearly a need for an order drafted in such a way as to give necessary powers in all circumstances in which a child might need protection in an emergency, the place of safety order which is an *ex parte* order, against which there is no right of appeal and which can last up to 28 days without parents having the right to access to their children or even to know where they are, is generally, as most recently demonstrated by the *Report of the Inquiry into Child Abuse in Cleveland* (Butler-Sloss, 1988), regarded as providing an unacceptable degree of overkill.

The order is, on the other hand, seen as less than adequate, in that it confers only limited powers on the local authority to have the child medically examined without the parents' consent, nor can the grounds, if strictly interpreted which they rarely are, look to the future (Ball, 1986b; Dyde, 1986; Blom-Cooper, 1985, 1987; CCLR, 1985).

Research evidence of the widespread misuse and over-use of place of safety orders in situations in which there is no immediate concern for a child's safety, but a perceived need to gain control of a situation, support misgivings as to the power the current provision places in the hands of social workers (Packman, 1986; Millham *et al.*, 1986). The White Paper proposal for an emergency protection order, available only on evidence of 'reasonable belief of damage to the child's health or well-being unless he can immediately be removed to or detained in a place of protection' and granted for an initial maximum of 8 days, with a possible extension of 7 days in exceptional circumstances, meets many of the objections to the latitude for abuse of the current order.

These proposals do not, however, satisfactorily address what may be described as the 'Kimberley Carlile factor', the need for powers to ensure that a social worker can insist on seeing a child about whom concern has been expressed, but to whom access is either denied or made difficult. The Committee into Kimberley's death recommends two additional powers for social workers to enable them to make adequate inquiries at a stage before there is evidence on which to ground an emergency protection order, or a section 40 warrant. Somewhat surprisingly since this was not an issue in Cleveland, Butler-Sloss in her report specifically rejected the need for such an order (Butler-Sloss, 1988).

Police powers

Children and Young Persons Act 1969 (s.28(2))
Under this section, a police officer may detain a child or young person if he has reasonable cause to believe that any of the primary conditions under s.1(2)(a)–(d) exist, or that a court would find (b) satisfied, or that a vagrant is taking the child about and thereby preventing his/her proper education. The case must be investigated by a senior police officer, who may either release the child or arrange for the child to be kept in a place of safety. Steps must be taken to inform the child and, if practicable, his/her parents or guardian of the reasons for detention, which can only be for a maximum of 8 days, and of the right to apply to a magistrate for the child's release (s.28(4)). Any detention beyond the initial 8 days can only be on application for an interim order.

There is considerable research evidence both of widespread variation in the incidence of use and under-recording of the making of police place of safety orders (Packman *et al.*, 1986; Millham *et al.*, 1986). Following recommendations in the *Child Care Law Review*, the government proposes reducing the length of time the police can hold juveniles in a place of safety to a maximum of 72 hours (CCLR, 1975; DHSS, 1987).

Police and Criminal Evidence Act 1984 (s.17(1)(e))
Although its application to child protection would be very unusual and restricted to cases of extreme emergency, the statutory provision restating the common law police power to enter and search any premises for the purpose of saving life or limb could be used in cases in which a child was, or was about to be, grossly physically abused (Blom-Cooper, 1987).

6 The child in care or under supervision

The general duty of local authorities to all children in care is laid down in the Child Care Act 1980 (s.18(1)):

> In reaching any decision relating to a child in their care, a local authority shall give first consideration to the need to safeguard and promote the welfare of the child throughout his childhood; and shall so far as is practicable ascertain the wishes and feelings of the child regarding the decision and give due consideration to them, having regard to his age and understanding.

In providing for children in care local authorities must make such use of the facilities and services provided for children in the care of their own parents as seems reasonable in each case (s.18(2)).

Under section 18(1), the general duty is subject to two provisions which reduce its overall effect. The local authority may exercise its powers in a way that is not consistent with its duty to consider the wishes and feelings of the child if this is necessary for protecting members of the public (s.18(3)). There is also a little-used power whereby, if the Secretary of State considers it necessary for the protection of the public, he may give directions to a local authority as to how it should deal with a particular case, and the local authority is bound to comply, even if the directions conflict with their general duty under section 18(1).

In principle, the local authorities' power over and duties towards all children in their care are the same, regardless of the route by which they entered; that is, they have all parental powers and duties, except the power to consent to adoption or to change the child's religion. In practice, this is not so. Although the local authority's duty towards children in voluntary care under section 2 of the 1980 Act is the same as their duty towards any other child in their care, the extent of their parental rights is limited by the voluntary nature of the arrangement; the child can always, unless made the subject of a parental rights resolution under section 3, be removed from care by a parent or guardian.

Care orders made in 'exceptional circumstances' in matrimonial or other proceedings impose some constraints on local authority decision-making, particularly as regards access and the discharge of orders (Cretney, 1984), and all major decisions concerning wards of court placed in local authority care have to be referred to the court for directions (Lowe and White, 1986, ch. 16; and see *Re C.B. (A Minor)* [1981]).

Local authorities' exercise of parental rights and duties centre on the key issues of where the child lives and where he/she goes to school; what access parents and others shall have to the child, and the child to them; and how local authorities review the child's situation and needs. Each needs separate consideration.

Placement

Local authorities have, subject to very detailed regulations regarding the boarding-out of children in care (Boarding out of Children Regulations 1989) and the constraints detailed above, absolute discretion as to where a child in care shall live, and are able to offer a wide range of possible placements: short- or long-term foster homes, community homes (with or without education on the premises), group homes, placement at home or with relatives and hostels and lodgings for older children about to leave care. The principles and practice implications of the choice of appropriate placement for a particular child are considered in detail elsewhere in this series (Thoburn, 1988).

The only legal, as opposed to practical, limitations on the local authorities' freedom of choice in respect of the accommodation of children in care is the constraint on their power to restrict personal liberty by locking up the child. Following a very active campaign through the European Court of Human Rights by the Children's Legal Centre, local authorities' previously unrestricted right to use secure accommodation without any reference to the courts was curtailed by means of amendments to the 1980 Act introduced in the Health and Social Services and Social Security Adjudications Act 1983.

Under section 21A(1) of the 1980 Act,

a child in the care of a local authority may not be placed, and if placed may not be kept, in accommodation provided for the purpose of restricting liberty unless it appears:

(a) that —
  (i) he has a history of absconding and is likely to abscond from any other type of accommodation; and
  (ii) if he absconds, it is likely that his physical, mental or moral welfare will be at risk; or
(b) that if he is kept in any other description of accommodation, he is likely to injure himself or other persons.

The Secretary of State has made a number of regulations under the Act, all of which are dependent on the above criteria being satisfied:

1. Children under the age of 10 cannot be locked up in a community home without prior approval from the Department of Health and Social Security (DHSS).
2. No child can be locked up for more than 72 hours in any 28-day period without the authority of a Juvenile Court. The juvenile must, unless he refuses it, be legally represented, and the parents must be notified of the application.
3. The court must authorize an initial period of up to 3 months and thereafter for periods of up to 6 months.
4. Children on remand may be locked up for the remand period but no longer (Secure Accommodation (No. 2) Regulations 1983).

Wards of court can only be placed in secure accommodation by direction of the judge (Secure Accommodation (No. 2) (Amendment) Regulations 1986). Where in wardship proceedings secure accommodation is being considered, a local authority circular (LAC 86/13) suggests that the child should be joined as a party to the proceedings in order to be properly represented. The case of every child kept in secure accommodation must be reviewed at least every 3 months by a panel appointed by the local authority for that purpose.

The education of children in care is clearly the legal responsibility of the local authority and one that has been woefully neglected in the past, both in social work practice and the literature (Jackson, 1987).

Parental access to children in care

In view of compelling research evidence of the extent to which the maintenance of contact between parents and their children in care is seen to be the most crucial factor in determining whether a child leaves care within a short time (Millham *et al.*, 1986), it is particularly unfortunate that it is an area in which the legal position of local authorities is so powerful, and that of parents so disadvantaged. It is unlikely that despite the excellent guide to good practice contained in the DHSS Code of Practice, *Access to Children in Care*, there will be any substantial improvement in this area until the legal imbalance is remedied by legislation.

Under the very limited access provisions hastily inserted, in 1983, into the 1980 Act as a result of pressure for reform following the House of Lords decision in *A.* v. *Liverpool City Council* [1982], parents whose access to their children in care has been terminated by the local authority may apply to the Juvenile Court for an access order. Up until notice of termination of access, or the refusal by the local authority to make any arrangements, parents have currently no means of challenging either the quantity or the quality of access.

The court when reaching its decision in access proceedings must apply the criteria laid down in the Guardianship of Minors Act 1971, that any court deciding issues relating to children 'shall regard the welfare of the minor as the first and paramount consideration'. Juvenile Courts when faced with evidence of the extent to which parents may have been disadvantaged by the local authority's practice over access to children have found it difficult to apply this test, and have had their decisions to make an access order under section 12(C) overturned on appeal (*Coventry City Council* v. *T.* [1986]). For judicial interpretation of the meaning of 'first and paramount' see *J.* v. *C.* [1970], *per* Lord MacDermott and *Re K.D. (A Minor: Access)* [1988], *per* Lord Oliver.

The parent(s) and the local authority are the parties in access proceedings; however, the court may, and usually does, decide that the child should be joined as a party and a guardian ad litem be appointed to safeguard his welfare, so that the court may have an independent social work view of the decision to terminate access; a step which in almost every case is a first move towards placing the child in a permanent substitute family by adoption. There is a real sense in which the Juvenile Court's decision in access proceedings may pre-empt a later decision to dispense with parental consent in adoption or freeing proceedings (see Chapter 7).

The White Paper proposals on parental access to children in care seek to reduce the current disadvantage suffered by parents by equating parental access to children in care to the access allowed the non-custodial parent in matrimonial proceedings. It is proposed that there will be a presumption of reasonable access which may be defined at the time the care order is made. The local authority will have to notify the parents of any intention to vary the existing access arrangements and the parents will be able to challenge the decision in court if they wish to do so (DHSS, 1987, para. 64).

Reviews

Local authorities have a general duty to review the cases of all children in their care every 6 months and to consider whether, if the child is subject to a care order, an application should be made to discharge the order (Children and Young Persons Act 1969, s.27(4)). In addition, long-term foster placements must be reviewed every 3 months and thereafter every 6 months (Boarding out of Children Regulations 1955, 22). There is substantial research evidence of wide disparity in the form, content and value of reviews, and a continuing debate about the part that parents and the children themselves play in them (McDonnell and Aldgate, 1984; Sinclair, 1984; Vernon and Fruin, 1986; Thoburn, 1988).

Children under local authority supervision
following care proceedings

A supervision order under section 11 of the 1969 Act, whether made in care or criminal proceedings, can be made for a maximum of 3 years, and puts the supervisor under general duty to advise, assist and befriend the supervised person (s.14).

In addition to the general requirement to keep in touch with the supervisor and inform him of any change of address or employment, a supervision order may include a number of requirements:

1. To reside with a named individual, who must agree (s.12(1)).
2. A requirement, which can only be made on the basis of medical evidence, to submit to treatment for mental disorder; a young person (over 14) must consent to such a requirement (s. 12B).
3. A requirement to 'comply with the directions of the supervisor' as set out in section 12(2). The words 'intermediate treatment' are not mentioned in the Act, but the provision by local authorities of a variety of programmes, including a short-term residential element, was central to the complete package in the 1969 Act. Intermediate treatment requirements under section 12(2) of the 1969 Act were not intended to be reserved for offenders and can be added to supervision orders made in care proceedings. Since the local authority decides the details of the activities in which it wishes the child to participate, these can prove very useful and flexible orders.

It should be noted that the requirement under section 12A(3) to participate in court-specified activities may only be added to supervision orders made in criminal proceedings (see Chapter 9).

The weakness of supervision orders made in care proceedings is that apart from an application to discharge that order and substitute a care order (s.15), there are no sanctions if the requirements in the order are not complied with. The 1987 White Paper proposes strengthening these supervision orders by allowing the court to impose requirements on parents or guardians rather than on the child (DHSS, 1987).

7 Adoption, custodianship and wardship

When children in local authority care are unable to be rehabilitated with their own parents or relatives, efforts will be made to ensure that they grow up in a permanent substitute family. For some, this will mean severance of all legal ties with their birth family and complete legal assimilation, through adoption, into a new one. For a few children, the less final, though ultimately less secure route, may be through custodianship.

Wardship comes at the end of the section on child care law because ultimately the jurisdiction can provide a safety net when all statutory provision fails to safeguard the welfare of the child, although its use in practice far exceeds this role.

Adoption

Adoption was first introduced into English law in 1926 with the objective of providing permanent and secure care in a family for orphan children or those whose natural parents were permanently unable or unwilling to bring them up. Under the Adoption of Children Act 1926 and all subsequent legislation, an adoption order effects a complete and virtually irrevocable legal transfer of a child from one family to another. While a detailed consideration of adoption law is beyond the scope of this book and those working in the field will need to make reference to a specialist work (Pearce, 1984; Bromley and Lowe, 1987), the legal issues surrounding adoption feature in many areas of child care practice.

Local authority social workers may be involved in adoption proceedings specifically because adoption may be being considered for children on their caseload or because they may have to prepare the very detailed report required by the court in all adoption cases under Schedule 2 of the Adoption Rules 1984. There is a sense in which all social workers are adoption workers since the Adoption Act 1976 places on all local authorities a statutory duty to:

> establish and maintain within their area a service designed to meet the needs in relation to adoption, of:
> (a) children who have been or may be adopted,
> (b) parents and guardians of such children, and
> (c) persons who have adopted or may adopt a child, and for that purpose to provide the requisite facilities, or secure that they are provided by approved adoption societies. (s.1(1))

The fact that the making of an adoption order effects such a profound change in a child's legal status is mirrored in the strict requirements laid down for all stages of the adoption process. An adoption order can — even if all the parties are agreeing — only be made by an authorized court, that is in the Magistrates' Domestic Court, the County Court or, in certain circumstances, the High Court. Currently the statutory provisions and procedural rules are to be found in the Adoption Act 1976, Adoption Rules, 1984 and the Adoption Agency Regulations 1983.

In order to ensure the 'normality' of the new family and that the child's welfare is the first consideration, the law provides strict requirements as to who may adopt or place for adoption, how the process is conducted, the consent or dispensing with the consent of the natural parents and how the interests of the child are both assessed by the agency and put before the court. An independent checking mechanism by the appointment of an independent reporting officer for the parents or where necessary a guardian ad litem to safeguard the welfare of the child is built into the system, to ensure that all the legal requirements have been met and that the order is in the child's interests.

At the heart of all the statutory provisions, but not over-riding any of the procedural rules, is the requirement that:

> the court or adoption agency shall have regard to all the circum-stances, the first consideration being given to the need to safeguard and promote the welfare of the child throughout his childhood; and shall so far as is practicable ascertain the wishes and feelings of the child regarding the decision and give due consideration to them, having regard to his age and understanding. (Adoption Act 1976, s.6)

Safeguarding the child's welfare may be better achieved by means of other procedures which make a less drastic alteration in his legal status than that effected by adoption, and such alternatives may have to be considered by social workers and the courts in many cases in which adoption is only one possible way of achieving permanence:

(a) In cases where the applicants are a parent and a step-parent, consideration must be given as to whether the matter would be better dealt with by variation of an existing custody order (Adoption Act 1976, s.14(3)), or where there has not been a previous marriage by a custodianship order under the Children Act 1975, s.33 (see below).

(b) In 'exceptional circumstances', having refused to make an adoption order, the court may make a supervision order in favour of a local authority or probation officer or commit the child to the care of the local authority (1976 Act, s.26).

Freeing for adoption

An adoption order is made, provided all the formalities are in order and the court decides that the making of the order is in the child's interests, following an application by the prospective adopters; the natural parents will have given their consent, or that consent will have been dispensed with by the court on one of the grounds set out in section 16 of the Act.

In cases in which either the child is already in the care of the agency and the issue of parental consent is in doubt, or where the mother wants the child adopted before any specific application is ready, the agency may apply to the court for an order freeing the child for adoption (s.18). The effect of the order, to which the parents must consent, or their consent be dispensed with, is to extinguish existing parental rights and vest them in the agency which will hold them until an adoption order is made. Natural parents will be informed if an order has been made or the child placed for adoption after a year, unless they sign a declaration that they do not wish to be further involved. If they have not signed the declaration and the child has not been placed, they may apply for revocation of the freeing order though this is rare indeed. Despite the considerable and desirable changes in adoption law that have been introduced since 1926 — mostly designed to equate the position of adopted children with natural children as regards legitimacy and inheritance, or as with the provisions introduced in the Children Act 1975, to discourage the somewhat artificial family structure resulting from adoption by step-parents — there is current concern over the extent to which legal provisions first conceived when almost all the children placed for adoption were illegitimate white babies, and most adopters childless couples, provide adequately for the very changed situation where increasingly the children are older and often coming to adoption with complex packages of previous relationships (Ball, 1987b; Hoggett, 1987).

Custodianship
A custodianship order under section 33 of the Children Act 1975 gives persons other than parents and those entitled to custody under the matrimonial or guardianship legislation legal custody of a child without the final severance of links with the original family effected by an adoption order. An account of the origins of the order and a detailed analysis of the custodianship provisions can be found elsewhere (Freeman, 1986; Pearce, 1986).

The award of legal custody means actual custody, together with 'so much of the parental rights and duties as relate to the person of the child' (1975 Act, s.86); the effect of this is that:

(a) the custodian makes all the day-to-day decisions in relation to the child;
(b) the order suspends but does not sever previous parental responsibility;
(c) a custodian may consent to medical treatment and to marriage but not to adoption, nor to emigration from the UK;
(d) children do not take their custodian's name without the consent of the parents or the court;
(e) the order lasts until the child is 18 years unless revoked before that date on application of the parents, the custodian or the local authority; it does not continue beyond the eighteenth birthday;

(f)   orders for access and maintenance may be attached to custodianship orders, and local authorities may pay means-tested allowances to custodians.

Local authorities have exactly the same rights and responsibilities in relation to children who are the subject of custodianship orders as they do in respect of any other children who are not in care, regardless of the child's legal status before the custodianship order was made.

The critical test to be applied by the courts in custodianship and ancillary proceedings is that laid down in section 1 of the Guardianship of Minors Act 1971. When an application is made in the Domestic or the County or the High Court by a 'suitable qualified applicant', as defined in section 33 of the 1975 Act, the local authority who will be a party to the proceedings must be notified by the applicant within 7 days. The authority has to prepare a report for the court which is almost identical to the Schedule 2 report in adoption proceedings, and includes information on the wishes and feelings of the child, the means and suitability of the applicant and the wishes and circumstances of the parents.

Custodianship as an alternative to adoption
Under section 37(1) of the 1975 Act, courts considering an adoption application by a parent and step-parent where there is no existing custody order have to be satisfied:

(a)   that the child's welfare would not be better safeguarded and promoted by the making of an adoption order in favour of the applicant than it would be by the making of a custodianship order in his favour; and
(b)   that it would be appropriate to make a custodianship order in the applicant's favour.

If this test is satisfied, the court can treat the application as being that of the step-parent only and make a custodianship order in their favour, but applicants clearly see custodianship as a poor alternative and the courts have interpreted the subsection as meaning that custodianship will only be the preferred alternative where it is clearly regarded as more appropriate than adoption (*Re S. (A Minor) (Adoption or Custodianship)* [1987]).

Carers as custodians

Until the implementation of the custodianship provisions, a *lacuna* existed in the law which could only be filled by wardship. Relatives and others who had looked after a child who was not an orphan, on an informal basis and possibly for many years, had no other recourse if a parent sought to reclaim the child. Since 1985 carers with whom the child has lived for 3 years may apply for custodianship, and the court will reach its decision solely on the basis of the child's welfare. In these circumstances neither parents nor local authorities may remove the child from the carers while an application is pending without the leave of the applicant or the court (s.41).

Custodianship was on the statute-book for ten years before the provisions were finally implemented in 1985. The shift that occurred in child care policy and practice during that decade towards adoption for children for whom it might not previously have been considered may partly account for the minimal use of custodianship by foster parents despite indications that many children would welcome being rid of the stigma and practical disadvantages of being in care. Other reasons speculated on include the financial reality that custodianship allowances are means-tested, whereas boarding out allowances are not, and foster parents' appreciation of some local authority support when dealing with difficult children. However, even if very few orders are being made, custodianship increases the range of planning options and may, for a few children, provide just the right route to permanence (Thoburn, 1988).

Wardship

'A ward of court is a child whose guardian is the High Court' (Law Commission, 1987); the effect of this is that whoever has day-to-day care and control of a ward, no important decision may be taken in his/her life without reference to the court; and the judge has the power to make infinitely flexible arrangements within the constraints of the criteria that all decisions have to recognize that the welfare of the child is paramount (Guardianship of Minors Act 1971, s.1).

The power of the High Court to assume guardianship of minors in need of protection, now primarily concerned with the welfare of children, stems from the ancient doctrine of *parens patriae* — the king as father of his people. It is a measure of the increasing part that wardship plays in the field of child care law that the jurisdiction has recently been subject to critical scrutiny by the Law Commission as part of the family law review of child care law (see Law Commission, 1987b).

The growth of the use of wardship by local authorities is a recent phenomenon. Almost all of the considerable rise in the numbers of originating summons in the last few years is accounted for by applications made by or with the agreement of local authorities, whose applications now make up 40 per cent of the total (Table 3).

Table 3   The incidence of originating summons in wardship (principal and district registries)

Year	Principal registry	District registry	Total
1971	622	n.a.	622
1981	822	1,081	1,903
1982	875	1,426	2,301
1983	802	1,338	2,140
1984	952	1,456	2,408
1985	965	1,850	2,815
1986	1,149	2,250	3,399

Source: Lowe and White, 1987; *Judicial Statistics*, 1986.

Wardship is a common law rather than a statutory jurisdiction; however, procedure in wardship cases is governed by the Supreme Court Act 1981 and the Rules of the Supreme Court (Order 90, rules 3–11). Under these rules, anyone with a declared personal or professional interest can make the child a ward of court by taking out an originating summons which has the immediate effect that, from that moment, no important step, such as leaving the country or moving residence or school or getting married or undergoing major surgery, may be taken without leave of the court. Unless an appointment for a hearing is made within 21 days, wardship lapses. If an appointment is made, the child continues to be a ward until the full hearing unless there is a successful interim application to de-ward (1981 Act, s.41).

The High Court has exclusive jursidiction to make a child a ward and to de-ward, but all intermediate decisions may now be transferred to and from the County Court in accordance with a practice direction (1986) of the President of the Family Division.

The child is not a party to wardship proceedings unless joined as such. Another practice direction restricts the types of case in which this may be appropriate to older children and exceptional cases (Practice Direction 1981). If the child is joined, a guardian ad litem must be appointed. This is often the Official Solicitor, who must be approached first, but he may authorize the continued involvement of a guardian ad litem panel member who has already been involved in care or access proceedings in the Juvenile Court and will therefore be familiar with the case. Such appointments which make a great deal of sense may not be without practical problems (Clarke, 1987; Butler-Sloss 1988) and seem likely to be discouraged (DHSS, 1988). If as is usually the case the child is not joined as a party, the judge may call for a report from a court welfare officer.

Social workers' main involvement with wardship will be when it is used by their authority as a means of securing the welfare of children already involved in concurrent proceedings in different courts, or for whom the usual statutory routes into care or provisions regarding parental access are seen as inappropriate or inadequate. Before considering that use of the jurisdiction in more detail, it may be helpful to outline other common types of situation, not involving local authorities, in which wardship is the only remedy.

Before implementation of the Child Abduction Act 1984, making the child a ward of court was the only means of activating the 'stop list' whereby all ports and airports are alerted to prevent the removal of a child from the jurisdiction, and wardship may still be useful in cases which fall outside the provisions of that Act.

As a result of the much-publicized case of Jeanette, it is now established that any proposed sterilization of a mentally handicapped minor requires the authority of a judge in wardship and such a decision can only be taken on the basis of the individual welfare of the girl in question (*Re B. (A Minor)*

(Wardship: Sterilization) [1987]). The issue of whether the High Court has an inherent jurisdiction to make similar decisions in respect of mentally handicapped adults is still unresolved, and is properly a matter for legislation. In addition, wardship can be used in disputes between parents and a recalcitrant teenager or in battles between themselves over their children, though the latter are rare because of the principal that legal aid will only extend to proceedings in the lowest court which is able to provide the remedy sought, in these circumstances the Domestic Court in proceedings under section 1(3) of the Guardianship Act 1973.

Local authorities' use of wardship

Wardship is immediate and the orders that may be made are infinitely flexible. However, as the Law Commission points out, many of the circumstances in which the jurisdiction is invoked by local authorities are or could be adequately provided for by statute, and the availability is unfairly weighted in favour of local authorities as against parents (Law Commission, 1987). This is because following a well-established legal principle, the High Court will not exercise its jurisdiction if this would conflict with local authorities' proper exercise of statutorily conferred discretionary powers such as those under the Child Care Act 1980, Part III, and the Children and Young Persons Act 1969 (*A.* v. *Liverpool City Council* [1982]).

The effect of this is that whereas local authorities can use wardship almost at will, parents, relatives and foster parents of children who are the subject of statutory proceedings, or in local authority care, are powerless to do so unless the local authority agrees to accept the jurisdiction. A guardian ad litem appointed in care proceedings and in dispute with the local authority over plans for the child is similarly prevented from invoking wardship (*A.* v. *Berkshire County Council* [1988]), although whether a guardian ad litem may do so to supplement the inadequate powers of justices is still in dispute (*Re T. (Minors)* [1988]).

There are several types of circumstances in which local authorities may choose to use wardship rather than proceedings in the Juvenile Court; the following list is not exclusive:

1. Where their route to an appeal is blocked in care or

discharge proceedings in order to get the justices' decision reviewed.
2. To bring within one jurisdiction cases in which there is a likelihood of concurrent proceedings concerning the same child in different courts.
3. To remove care proceedings from the Juvenile Court, either because of lack of confidence in a local court or the likely length and complexity of the case makes it more suitable for hearing by an experienced judge on the basis of affidavit evidence (Lowe and White, 1987, p. 62).
4. To ensure that the local authority's powers under a care order are supplemented by the power of the High Court to issue injunctions (*Re J.J. (A Minor) (Wardship: Committal to Care)* [1986]).

The Law Commission in their Working Paper on wards of court (Law Commission, 1987b) question whether the wardship jurisdiction will continue to be justified when the private law of child care is reformed according to their proposals and administered within a family court with a unified jurisdiction. That utopia is some way off. For the present, the wardship jurisdiction seems likely to continue to exist to fill in the gaps in the statutory provision and avoid the inadequacy of some courts, despite its availability being unfairly but inevitably 'limited to local authorities and a small number of comparatively well off or unusually determined litigants' (Hoggett, 1987, p. 161).

PART III
THE LEGAL CONTEXT OF WORK
WITH OTHER CLIENT GROUPS

8 Aspects of disability: mental disorder, the handicapped and elderly

Mentally disordered people

A more detailed knowledge of mental health law is required by those appointed as approved social workers under the Mental Health Act 1983 than can be provided by a general text such as this and several specialist texts are available (Hoggett, 1984; Rashid and Ball, 1987; Gostin, Meacher and Olsen, 1983). In addition, an historical perspective such as that provided by Hoggett is necessary not only to appreciate the dramatic changes that have occurred this century in the statutory framework which determines the limits of intervention in the lives of mentally disordered people, but also to understand much of the present legislation. All local authority social workers, even if not authorized to exercise them, need to be aware of the statutory powers that exist in relation to the mentally ill and handicapped and the legal restraints that should prevent abuse of those powers.

The law relating to the treatment of mentally disordered patients in England and Wales is contained in the Mental Health Act 1983, which consolidated much of the 1959 Mental Health Act with substantial amendments introduced in the Mental Health (Amendment) Act 1982. Although the provisions of the 1983 Act differ substantially in detail from those of the 1959 Act, the principle on which treatment is provided — the innovative cornerstone of the earlier Act — has not altered:

> Nothing in this Act shall be construed as preventing a patient who requires treatment for mental disorder from being admitted to any hospital or nursing home in pursuance of arrangements made in that behalf and without any application, order or direction rendering him liable to be detained under this Act or from remaining in any

hospital or mental nursing home in pursuance of such arrangements after he has ceased to be so liable to be detained. Mental Health Act 1983, s.131(1))

The powers to admit or detain mentally disordered people in hospital compulsorily can only be considered when all attempts to persuade the patient to accept treatment on a voluntary basis have failed, and then only in circumstances which meet the detailed requirements set out in the Act.

Definitions under the 1983 Act

The legislation refers 'to the reception, care and treatment of mentally disordered patients'. Under section 1(2), *mental disorder* means mental illness (which is not defined in the legislation), arrested or incomplete development of mind, psychopathic disorder and any other disorder or disability of mind.

Severe mental impairment means a state of arrested or incomplete development of mind which includes severe impairment of intelligence and social functioning and is associated with abnormally aggressive or seriously irresponsible conduct on the part of the person concerned.

Mental impairment means a state of arrested or incomplete development of mind (not amounting to severe mental impairment) which includes significant impairment of intelligence and social functioning and is associated with abnormally aggressive or seriously irresponsible conduct of the person concerned.

Psychopathic disorder means a persistent disorder or disability of mind, whether or not including significant impairment of intelligence, which results in abnormally aggressive or seriously irresponsible conduct on the part of the person concerned.

It is important to note that severe mental impairment, mental impairment and psychopathic disorder all require evidence of 'abnormally aggressive or seriously irresponsible conduct', and that behaviour due solely to promiscuity or immoral conduct, sexual deviancy, drugs or alcohol dependence is excluded from the definition of mental disorder (s.1(3)).

Approved social workers
The role and responsibilities of social workers working with
the mentally ill were both enhanced and extended by the
1983 Act. As from October 1984, only approved social
workers (ASWs) appointed and approved by their authorities
'as having appropriate competence in dealing with persons
suffering from mental disorder' can carry out duties under
the Act. The post-qualifying training requirement for ASWs
involves a programme of at least 60 days' training (CCETSW,
1987).

The powers and duties of the ASW include interviewing
patients in a suitable manner; making applications for
admissions to hospital or helping nearest relative to do so;
applying to the County Court to replace the nearest relative
when that relative is preventing on grounds the ASW
considers unreasonable the patient's removal to hospital
(*W. v. L.* [1974]); conveying patients to hospital; entering
and inspecting premises in which a mentally disordered
person is living; and if necessary, applying for a warrant to
search for and remove the patient (s. 135(1)) (see Hoggett,
1984; Rashid and Ball, 1987).

Nearest relatives
Relatives are defined under section 26 of the Mental Health
Act 1983 with the 'nearest' higher on the list with the oldest
in any category taking precedence regardless of sex:

— husband or wife;
— son or daughter;
— father or mother;
— brother or sister;
— grandparent;
— grandchild;
— uncle or aunt;
— nephew or niece.

In practice, there are further extensions; for instance, a cohabitee may be regarded as a spouse after 6 months, and
where there are no other relations, after five years a non-
relative fellow lodger or landlady may be considered a
relative for the purposes of the Act (Hoggett, 1984).

Compulsory powers
There are three procedures for applying for compulsory admission to hospital, without judicial proceedings, on the application of the nearest relative or an approved social worker supported by the recommendation of one or two doctors, and one – rarely used – for guardianship in the community. A patient already in hospital may become subject to compulsory detention on the basis of a report by the doctor in charge of his case, or in more extreme circumstances by a nurse. In addition, the police have the power to remove to a place of safety any person found in a public place who appears to be suffering from a mental disorder and to be in need of care or control, and an approved social worker (ASW) can apply for a warrant to authorize the police to enter premises to search for a mentally disordered person and, if necessary, remove them to a safe place.

The courts, or the Home Secretary, may make orders under the Act compulsorily detaining patients who have been accused of criminal offences. Each of these powers, or 'sections' as they are commonly known, need to be looked at separately.

Admission for assessment   Section 2 of the 1983 Act authorizes the detention of the patient for up to 28 days on an application by the nearest relative or someone authorized by them or by the County Court to act on their behalf, or by an approved social worker, supported by recommendations from two doctors, one of whom must be an approved specialist in mental disorder and both of whom must have examined the patient either together or within 5 days of each other. The medical recommendation must be based on the fact that the patient

  (a) is suffering from mental disorder of a nature or degree which warrants the detention of the patient in a hospital for assessment (or for assessment followed by treatment) for at least a limited period; and
  (b) he ought to be so detained in the interests of his own safety or with a view to the protection of other persons.

The applicant is responsible for getting the patient to hospital, and may seek help from the ambulance service or the police. If patients escape, they may be apprehended and returned, but after 14 days from the date of the second medical recommendation authority to detain or admit the patient lapses. If patients reach the hospital within 14 days, authority to detain them lasts for 28 days unless steps are taken to detain for further treatment.

An order for discharge may be made in respect of a patient detained for assessment by the responsible medical officer, the managers or the nearest relative. If the patient applies to a Mental Health Review Tribunal within 14 days of admission to hospital, the tribunal may discharge the patient.

Admission for assessment in an emergency   In an emergency an application for assessment may be made with the support of only one doctor, who need not be a mental health specialist, though he should if possible have previous acquaintance with, and must have examined, the patient within the 24 hours prior to the patient's removal to hospital (s.4).

An emergency application, which authorizes detention for up to 72 hours, may be made either by the nearest relative or by an approved social worker. The application must not only state that it is 'of urgent necessity for the patient to be admitted and detained', but be supported by a statement from the recommending doctor indicating the length of the delay that would be caused by obtaining a second medical opinion, why this might result in harm and whether the harm would be caused to the patient or to those caring for the patient or to other people (Mental Health (Hospital Guardianship and Consent to Treatment) Regulations 1983, Form 7). After 72 hours, authority to detain the patient lapses, unless a second medical recommendation (made if the initial one was not) by a doctor 'approved as having special experience in the diagnosis or treatment of mental disorder' converts the emergency admission into a section 2 (28 days) admission.

Emergency procedures as introduced by the provisions of the Mental Health Act 1959 (s.29) were originally intended for exceptional use only. As with other similar provisions where the emergency procedure is either less complicated, or less demanding in terms of evidence, in practice the procedure intended for occasional emergency use became the normal route. This gave rise to considerable concern among those working with the mentally ill (Gostin, 1975, 1978; DHSS, 1976).

Under the 1983 Act, use of the procedure has been discouraged, in that the categories of person who make application for an emergency admission are restricted to nearest relatives and approved social workers. At the same time, stricter criteria for invoking the procedure were introduced and their observance encouraged by the regulations. It is a matter for continuing criticism, however, that patients can still be admitted under section 4 on a medical recommendation given by a doctor who may have no prior knowledge of the patient, nor any experience or expertise in the diagnosis of mental disorder (Hoggett, 1984, ch. 4).

Admission for treatment (s.3)   An application for admission for treatment under this section may be made by the nearest relative or, if the nearest relative objects, someone appointed by the County Court to act as such or, with the agreement of the nearest relative, by an ASW. The applicant must have seen the patient within the previous 14 days and the application must be supported by recommendations by two doctors, one of them an approved specialist, to the effect that the patient

(a) is suffering from mental illness, severe mental impairment, psychopathic disorder or mental impairment and his mental disorder is of a nature or degree which makes it appropriate for him to receive medical treatment in a hospital; and

(b) in the case of a psychopathic disorder or mental impairment, such treatment is likely to alleviate or prevent a deterioration of his condition; and

(c) it is necessary for the health and safety of the patient or for the protection of other persons that he should receive such treatment and it cannot be provided unless he is detained under this section.

The patient may then be detained, in the first instance, for up to 6 months, then for a further 6 months and thereafter for a year at a time on the basis of a report from the responsible medical officer (RMO) to the hospital managers which states that continued detention is necessary using the same criteria as those justifying the initial admission.

Subject to certain safeguards, many forms of treatment

except those which are irreversible may be administered to patients admitted or detained under section 3 without their consent, provided that a second medical opinion is sought (see also sections 57 and 58, and Hoggett, 1984).

While a patient is detained for treatment under section 3, discharge may be by the RMO, the managers or the nearest relative. If the RMO certifies that 'the patient if discharged would be likely to act in a manner dangerous to other persons or to himself' (s.25(d)), discharge by the nearest relative may be blocked. In those circumstances, the nearest relative can apply to a Mental Health Review Tribunal. The patient may also apply to be discharged by a Mental Health Review Tribunal within the first 6 months of detention and once during each subsequent period of renewal.

Patients already in hospital (s.5)   If it appears to the registered medical practitioner in charge of the medical treatment of a voluntary in-patient that an application ought to be made for the patient's detention in hospital, he may provide the managers with a report in writing to that effect and the patient may be detained in hospital for 72 hours from the time the report was furnished. Under section 5(4), a nurse may, if no practitioner is available, furnish a report to the managers to record that fact in writing and the patient may be detained for up to 6 hours (s.5(4)).

Detention in a 'place of safety' (s.136)   A police officer finding a person who appears to be suffering from mental disorder, and to be in need of care or control, in a public place may remove that person to a place of safety if he thinks it necessary in their interests or for the safety of others. The section authorizes detention for up to 72 hours for the purpose of medical and social work assessment, the patient most usually being detained in a police station or hospital. Use and possible abuse of the section have attracted attention from researchers and those concerned with the rights of the mentally ill. Although the powers are not widely used outside London, there is evidence of considerable under-recording (Butler, 1975) and some pressure from MIND during the debate on the 1982 Amendment Act both to tighten the criteria and reduce the detention period to a maximum of 24 hours (Gostin, 1975).

Police warrant under s.135(1)   An ASW who has reason to believe that a mentally disordered person is not under proper care may apply to a magistrate for a warrant which will empower a police officer accompanied by an ASW and a doctor to enter premises, by force if necessary, and again if it is considered necessary to remove the mentally disordered person to a place of safety without formally 'sectioning' the person for up to 72 hours. There is no power to treat the patient without his/her consent under this procedure. Definitions under this section are difficult and there is some suspicion that its apparent very low rate of use masks considerable flouting of the law by the professionals involved (Hoggett, 1984).

Guardianship   When the 1959 Act was implemented, it was envisaged that compulsory care within the community would replace hospital orders for most patients. In fact only a minute number of guardianship orders were made. The 1983 Act provisions attempt to make guardianship more workable, though there is as yet little indication that many orders, either civil or criminal, are being made.

The rules as to the applicants and medical recommendations are similar to those for compulsory admission to hospital; the application is addressed to the local authority, and the proposed guardian may be an individual approved by the local authority who consents to act or any social service authority which accepts responsibility. Under the 1983 Act, the guardian has the power to:

(i)   require the patient to reside at a place specified;
(ii)   attend at places and times specified for the purpose of medical treatment, occupation, etc.;
(iii) require that access to the patient may be given to any doctor, ASW or other similar person.

Under the Act, patients may be transferred from hospital to guardianship and vice versa. The duration and termination of guardianship orders are very similar to those for patients admitted for treatment under section 3 (Rashid and Ball, 1987).

Orders made in criminal proceedings
Remands and interim orders under sections 35, 36 and 38 were introduced into the 1983 Act to provide for those cases in which a remand on bail with a condition of psychiatric assessment is considered impracticable, but the alternative of prison does not provide a suitable environment for such an assessment. This is an important issue for probation officers who may need to write social inquiry reports on mentally disordered offenders for whom use of these provisions may be appropriate (Stone, 1988).

Remand to hospital for a report (s.35) Any person awaiting trial for an offence (except murder) punishable with imprisonment may, if the court is satisfied on medical evidence that there is reason to suggest that the accused is suffering from mental illness, psychopathic disorder, severe mental impairment (the four categories), may be remanded to a specified hospital with a bed available within 7 days for a 'report on his mental condition'. The remand may be for up to 28 days and is renewable for similar periods up to a total of 12 weeks. Offenders detained under this section cannot be compelled to accept treatment.

Remand of an accused person for treatment (s.36) Persons accused of offences punishable with imprisonment (excluding murder) who are certified by two registered medical practitioners to be suffering from 'mental illness or severe mental impairment of a nature or degree which makes it appropriate for them to be detained in hospital for treatment' may be remanded to hospital for treatment, which under this section cannot be refused.

Interim hospital orders (s.38) This section provides for a convicted offender to be made the subject of an interim hospital order on the evidence of two registered medical practitioners that the offender is suffering from one of the four categories of mental disorder and that 'there is reason to suppose that the disorder from which the defendant is suffering is such that it may be appropriate for a hospital order to be made in his case'.
This order authorizes admission to hospital within 28 days for an initial period of 12 weeks, which may be increased by

periods of up to 28 days to a maximum of 6 months, provided that the offender's legal representative is heard if extensions are made.

Hospital or guardianship order (s.37)   A hospital order, which has the effect of an admission for treatment under section 3, may be made by a court sentencing for an imprisonable offence (except murder) on evidence of two registered medical practitioners of the existence of one of the four categories of mental disorder. If an order is made under section 37, the nearest relative does not have the power to discharge the patient, only to apply to the Mental Health Review Tribunal on the patient's behalf after 6 months; patients may make a similar application on their own behalf. The condition must be likely to respond to treatment or warrant guardianship, and the court must consider the order the most appropriate method of disposing of the case (for greater detail and a commentary, see Hoggett, 1984).

Restriction order (s.41)

> Where a hospital order is made in respect of an offender by the Crown Court and it appears to the court having regard to the nature of the offence, the antecedents of the offender, and the risk of his committing further offences if set at large that it is necessary for the protection of the public from serious harm so to do, the court may . . . order that the offender be subject to the special restriction set out in this section.

The restriction order can only be made in the Crown Court and has the effect of limiting the power to order discharge to the secretary of state, who has to receive annual reports on the offender, or a Mental Health Review Tribunal. Discharge, when authorized, may be absolute or conditional (Rashid and Ball, 1987, ch. 4). Probation officers also need to be aware of the power that exists to allow the transfer of mentally disordered prisoners to hospital under sections 47 and 48 with possible restriction under section 49 (Stone, 1988).

Mental Health Review Tribunals
Mental Health Review Tribunals provide an independent specialist forum before which almost all compulsorily

detained patients can have their detention reviewed. There is a Tribunal for each regional health authority and each panel has legal, medical and lay members 'who have such experience in administration, such knowledge of social services or such other qualifications and experience as the Lord Chancellor considers suitable'. A tribunal is made up of at least one member of each group with a lawyer presiding. Hoggett (1984) considers in detail the various applications that may be made to tribunals and the different procedures that apply.

The Court of Protection

Mentally disordered people, whether they are in hospital or not, may not be able to manage their own affairs and may be vulnerable to exploitation. If a mentally incapable person owns even a small amount of property, it is likely that the powers of the Court of Protection may have to be invoked. This court, which is an office of the Supreme Court, exists solely to deal with the affairs of people who are incapable of managing for themselves.

Proceedings in the Court of Protection are usually started by the patient's nearest relative by means of an originating application, but anyone can apply and social workers may find themselves needing to do so on behalf of a client. Before the court can intervene, it has to have a certificate from a registered medical practitioner that the patient is incapable by reason of medical disorder from conducting his own affairs, and either a simple certificate if the patient's income is under £1,000 and capital under £5,000 or, if larger amounts are involved, a sworn affidavit setting out particulars of property and affairs, details of relatives and the grounds for making the application.

The patient must be served with notice of the application or, if the matter is simple, the proposed summary order unless the court considers that the person is incapable of understanding. After that, the patient has at least 7 days or until the date of the hearing, whichever is later, in which to object in writing to the court. There is no provision for a patient to be heard in person.

The court can make any relative or anyone else who seems interested in the application a party to the proceedings, and any relative closer than the applicant should be informed. All this can take a considerable time; however, if there is urgent need for immediate protection, the court can make such interim orders as it considers necessary.

Once a patient is subject to the court's jurisdiction, it has exclusive control over all the person's property and affairs and wide powers to fulfil this function for the maintenance and benefit of the patient and family. Unless the patient's affairs are sufficiently straightforward to be dealt with by a simple order, the court will appoint a receiver, who will be empowered in very precise terms to protect the estate and use it for the patient's behalf and will have to render annual accounts. The receiver may be a relative, professional adviser or any other suitable person who is prepared to act. If there is no such individual, the Official Solicitor may be appointed.

The powers of the Court of Protection are massive and its procedures both cumbersome and expensive, in that not insubstantial fees deducted from the patient's property are charged. However, its powers provide protection from exploitation which cannot be achieved in any other way. The court's functions continue until the patient dies or, exceptionally, the court finds that it can discharge the receiver because patients have recovered sufficiently to manage their own affairs. Other less intrusive but correspondingly less effective measures which may be taken in regard to the affairs of mentally incapable people have been discussed elsewhere (Ball, 1988a).

The physically handicapped and elderly

Local authorities have a general power under section 29 of the National Assistance Act 1948 to make arrangements to promote the welfare of disabled people, to provide housing (Part III) and a duty under the Chronically Sick and Disabled Persons Act 1970 to inform themselves of the level of need within their area and to keep a register of disabled persons. Under the as yet only partially implemented Disabled Persons (Services, Consultation and Representation) Act 1986, disabled persons or their carers may ask the local authority to assess through an elaborate procedure (s.3) a disabled person's needs for services and the local authority has to make a decision.

The main problem with all the legislation relating to disabled people is that it provides an enabling framework for good practice but that few provisions are mandatory. This is particularly the case with the 1970 Act, which has failed to live up to the high hopes of those responsible for its introduction. Statutory provision to meet the particular needs of disabled persons are considered in outline by Rashid and Ball (1987) and in practical detail in the *Disability Rights Handbook* (Annual).

Compulsory removal from home

The compulsory removal from home of an elderly, infirm or chronically sick person who does not come within the terms of the Mental Health Act 1983, although it may occasionally be necessary in their interests, involves grave issues of civil liberties (Alison, 1980; Tinker, 1985).

An order authorizing removal from home on these grounds can only be obtained from a court, or in an emergency *ex parte* from a single justice, if the statutory criteria are met. The power of removal under section 47(1) of the National Assistance Act 1948 applies only to persons who:

(a) are suffering from grave chronic disease or, being aged, infirm or physically incapacitated, are living in insanitary conditions, and

(b) are unable to devote to themselves, and are not receiving from other persons, proper care and attention.

The court procedure requires the Community Health Officer to certify in writing to the local authority that he is satisfied that an order is necessary. The local authority may apply to a Magistrates' Court for an order, which provided the court is satisfied that one is necessary, is limited to 3 months and extendable by another 3 months. The patient must be given 7 days' notice of the hearing and any hospital 7 days' notice of the arrival of the patient. The patient or anyone on their behalf may, having given 7 days' notice to the local authority, apply for discharge of the order after 6 weeks.

An emergency procedure, which as with admission for assessment under the Mental Health Act 1959 (s.29) has become the norm, was introduced by section 1 of the National Assistance (Amendment) Act 1951. Under this procedure, the local authority may make an *ex parte* application on the grounds set out in section 47(1) of the 1948

Act to a Magistrates' Court or single justice. The Community
Health Officer and another registered medical practitioner,
usually the patient's general practitioner, have to certify
that in their opinion, 'it is necessary in the interests of that
person to remove him without delay' (1951 Act, s.1(1)).
Under this procedure, the initial period of detention is for
3 weeks.

When anyone is admitted to hospital under the above
provisions or into accommodation provided under Part III of
the 1948 Act, the local authority has a statutory responsibility to take reasonable steps to mitigate loss or damage,
and under section 48(2) of the 1948 Act, has a power of
entry to the previous place of residence in order to carry
out this duty. Local authorities have detailed procedures to
be followed by workers to ensure that their responsibilities
under this section are met.

9 Juvenile offenders and the Juvenile Court

Background
Special Magistrates' Courts for juvenile offenders were first set up under the Children Act 1908 to provide procedures more suitable for children and to protect juveniles from contact with, and contamination by, adult offenders. The law relating to criminal proceedings in the Juvenile Court is currently contained in the Children and Young Persons Acts of 1933 and 1969 as considerably amended, and procedure in the Juvenile Court is governed by the Magistrates' Courts (Children and Young Persons) Rules 1988.

From the beginning, courts for young offenders were also given jurisdiction over juveniles who were thought to be in need of care, thus starting the elision of welfare and justice which still causes confusion as to the exact nature of both care and criminal proceedings in the Juvenile Court (CCLR, 1985; Anderson, 1978). The growth first of the welfare model of juvenile justice, its subsequent fall from favour and the current state of uncertainty as to the ideological basis of juvenile justice in England and Wales has most recently been usefully and comprehensively considered, albeit from a partial 'justice' position, by Morris and Giller (1987). If anything is certain in the juvenile justice system, it is that there is an infinite variety of practice and interpretation of court procedure throughout the whole system from the initial police involvement to the court's sentencing decisions (Anderson, 1978; Ball, 1983; Parker, Casburn and Turnbull, 1981; Priestley, Fears and Fuller, 1977; NACRO, 1984, 1988b).

Constitution of the Juvenile Court
The lay justices who sit in the Juvenile Court are elected to the juvenile panel for a three-year term by all the magistrates

in their petty sessional division, or are selected by the Lord Chancellor for the Inner London panel. They should normally be under the age of 50 when first appointed and have experience of dealing with young people and 'a real appreciation of the surroundings and way of life of the children who are likely to come before the courts' (HO Circular, 1979). The extent to which these requirements are met varies greatly depending on the policies of the individual bench and on the availability of suitable candidates. Juvenile panel justices are expected to undertake some additional training and are encouraged to visit community homes run by local authorities and prison service establishments for juvenile offenders.

It is a continuing cause for official concern that in some areas the juvenile panels are too large for the amount of work, with the result that individual members are unable to 'obtain sufficient practical experience of this important and specialised work' (HO Circular, 1979). Recent research shows some evidence of a reduction in the size of panels relative to their sittings, and of an increase in the number of panels made up of a combination of justices from several Petty Sessional Divisions (PSDs) within one clerkship (NACRO, 1988b).

In order to avoid those appearing in the Juvenile Court coming into contact with adult offenders, the Rules provide that juvenile courts should be held, where possible, in a different building or on a different day from adult courts; at the very least, the Juvenile Court may not be held in the same room in which an adult court has sat or will sit within one hour (1933 Act, s.47(2)). Arrangements have to be made for separate waiting-areas for those attending Juvenile Courts. The physical settings in which Juvenile Courts are held and the suitability of the facilities available vary as randomly as all other aspects of the juvenile justice system (Hilgendorf, 1981).

Jurisdiction of the Juvenile Court

Care and access proceedings
The Juvenile Court has sole first-instance jurisdiction in all care and discharge proceedings under the Children and Young Persons Act 1969, access proceedings under the Child Care

Act 1980 (s.12(A)–(F)) and parental rights proceedings under the 1980 Act (s.3) (see Chapter 5).

Criminal proceedings
There is no criminal responsibility for persons under 10 years of age. Children aged 10–13, and young persons aged 14–16, will have all criminal charges against them heard in the Juvenile Court, except where:

1. the charge is one of homicide (1933 Act, s.53(1));
2. a young person is charged with an offence for which the maximum penalty in the case of an adult is 14 years' imprisonment, and the circumstances of the offence are such that a substantial penalty is required, the young person may be committed to the Crown Court for trial (1933 Act, s.53(2));
3. the juvenile is jointly charged with an adult;
4. the juvenile appears in the adult court because of a mistake as to his age.

In the last two circumstances above, the Magistrates' Court may deal with the case by way of discharge or fine; if it wishes to impose a greater penalty, it must remit the case to the Juvenile Court for sentence unless the juvenile is committed to the Crown Court under section 53(2). Use of this section has more than doubled within the past decade, from 65 in 1980 to 156 in 1988. This and other important anomalies about the use of the provision are addressed in the report of a NACRO Working Group (NACRO, 1988a).

Arrest and the criminal process
Juveniles arrested by the police have rights regarding arrest and interrogation under the Police and Criminal Evidence Act 1984, in addition to those for adults described in Chapter 4:

1. Juveniles may not be arrested or interviewed at school, except in exceptional circumstances (1984 Act, Code C, para. 13D).
2. When a juvenile is brought to a police station under arrest, the custody officer must contact the 'appropriate adult' (parent or social worker) and ask them to attend

the police station; questioning of the juvenile must not begin before the adult arrives unless authorized in cases of grave urgency by a superintendent or officer above (s.13.1).

3. Juveniles, like adults, must be informed of their right to have a solicitor present at the police station; if the appropriate adult considers that legal advice should be taken, interrogation must not start until such advice has been obtained.

4. Juveniles should not be detained in police cells unless there is nowhere else they can be properly supervised (C8).

5. The rules relating to the fingerprinting of juveniles are outlined in Chapter 4.

Remand   If a juvenile is charged, he must normally be released on bail, or may be remanded to the care of the local authority. Boys of 15 and 16 charged with offences carrying a maximum penalty of 14 years' imprisonment may, if the Juvenile Court certifies that they are too unruly, be remanded instead to a remand centre or prison. Annually about 1,500 boys, a substantial proportion of whom subsequently receive a non-custodial penalty, are remanded to penal establishments. A recent proposal in the form of a Home Office consultative paper to introduce stricter criteria for the issue of unruliness certificates was generally widely welcomed, but met with determined opposition from magistrates and justices' clerks.

Legal aid is available in the Juvenile Court subject to parental means and the same criteria as in the adult court, except that legal representation must be offered when care or custodial sentences are being considered, unless the defendant refuses to apply for legal aid or to consult a solicitor.

Diversion from the criminal process

As with all aspects of the juvenile justice system, the process whereby a juvenile who is arrested or reported by the police for committing a criminal offence receives a caution or appears before the Juvenile Court varies widely depending on the locality (Priestley, Fears and Fuller, 1977). Most police authorities have some form of juvenile liaison scheme or juvenile bureau which operates with the co-operation of the probation, social and education welfare services to divert many offending juveniles, who admit their offences, away from court by means of a formal police caution. Rates of caution vary widely from one police authority to another but have, on the whole, risen steadily over the past decade (Tutt and Giller, 1983).

Procedure in court
When a juvenile does appear in court, the procedure followed is a modified version of that for an adult. It is designed to give the defendant the protection of due process, but also to allow parents to have an opportunity to make their views known to the court. Statutorily the Juvenile Court is bound to 'have regard to the welfare of the child' when reaching a decision (1933 Act, s.44), yet that duty does not prevent the court from reaching decisions and imposing penalties which may be clearly contrary to the child's interests but which the justices may believe necessary for the protection of the public.

As in summary proceedings in the adult court, the defendant in the Juvenile Court is entitled to a summary of the evidence against him if the offence is indictable or one triable either way in the case of an adult (Magistrates' Courts (Advance Information) Rules 1985).

Although many would question whether they achieve their objective, the procedural rules which govern Juvenile Court proceedings seek to avoid undue stigma and publicity while maintaining the important principle of open justice. Attendance in court is restricted to those involved in the case and the press, who may publish reports of the proceedings but not any details, such as name, address or school, which might identify the defendant, unless the court rules that it is in the interests of justice that they should be made public. At least one parent or guardian is summoned to attend court with the juvenile unless the court exercises its discretion not to require an adult to attend as it may, for instance, in the case of 16-year-olds charged with minor motoring offences, who were they adult could plead guilty by letter (Ball, 1981b).

The actual hearing follows only a slightly modified version of adult proceedings, in that the charge must be expressed in simple language and an opportunity given to the parents to express their view as to the propriety of the plea. If there is any doubt whether or not the defendant should admit the offence, the court should err on the side of caution and record a denial. In addition, there is provision for a juvenile to change his plea at any time before the final order is made (S. v. *Recorder of Manchester* [1971]).

If the juvenile denies the offence, the trial will follow the normal pattern, with attempts — often not very successful — being made to ensure that an unrepresented juvenile is helped with the cross-examination of prosecution witnesses and other problems of evidence. If the charge is admitted, or after a finding of guilt, the court proceeds to sentence; and at this stage, the court will be made aware of any previous cautions or findings of guilt and will read any reports presented by the local authority.

Reports for the court

Under section 9(1) of the 1969 Act, where children are brought before the Juvenile Court by the local authority in care or, in criminal proceedings, the police, it is stated:

> It shall be the duty of the authority, unless they are of the opinion that it is necessary to do so, to make such investigation and provide the court before which the proceedings are heard with such information relating to the home surroundings, school record, health and character of the person in respect of whom the proceedings are brought as appear to the authority likely to assist the court.

This wording gives local authorities considerable discretion as to whether reports should be prepared and as to their content.

Until recently, it was the practice in all except very minor or motoring cases for social inquiry reports prepared by social services or the probation service, and a report from the offender's school, either to be routinely prepared in advance of the hearing, unless it was known that the charge was being denied, or for the case to be adjourned for reports. During the past decade considerable research-based disquiet has been expressed about the possibility that the content of reports on many juveniles committing minor offences was resulting in effectively more severe sentences than was warranted by their offending behaviour (Thorpe *et al.*, 1980; Morris *et al.*,

1980). This evidence combined with policy decisions in the probation service to target their limited resources to providing non-custodial alternatives for serious offenders at risk of custody, and to restrict report-writing to those cases, has with the support of social service departments led to a very marked reduction in the numbers of reports presented to the Juvenile Court (NACRO, 1988b).

This reduction has been achieved, in many areas, by agreement between the juvenile panel and the agencies that reports will not be required for those appearing before the court for the first or possibly second time unless the offence is so serious that the court might be considering a custodial penalty. If in any particular case the court is unwilling to proceed to sentence without the background information which reports would provide, it always has the power under section 9(2) of the 1969 Act to request reports or further information, and unlike the initial provision under subsection 1, the local authority has no discretion; it must comply with the request.

It is apparent that, in many areas, the reduction of the numbers of social inquiry reports (SIRs) prepared has not been matched by a reduction in school reports, which recent research evidence shows are often routinely prepared when an SIR would only be available on request after an adjournment (NACRO, 1988b). This gives rise to concern because of evidence of the possible undue influence of educational factors, as brought to the courts' attention through the school court report, on the outcome of criminal proceedings in the Juvenile Court (Ball, 1981; Sumner *et al.*, 1988). One of the recommendations in the second NACRO Report on school reports in the Juvenile Court is that this practice should end and that reports from schools should only be prepared and presented with SIRs, ideally in a single document (NACRO, 1988b).

Many of the larger Juvenile Courts have an arrangement with the agencies, much favoured by justices, that in cases in which the bench is reluctant to proceed without any background information, a social worker or probation officer will if the case is adjourned for a short time be available to interview the defendant and his parents and provide the court with a 'stand-down' report as to whether they consider an adjournment for a full report to be necessary.

When reports are presented in Juvenile Court proceedings, they are subject to procedural rules which partly as a result of research evidence, and pressure mounted by NACRO (1984), have recently been revised to allow parents and defendants access to the contents of all reports (Magistrates' Courts (Children and Young Persons) Rules 1988, rule 10(2)), with provision to exclude defendants in very limited circumstances. This not only removes a considerable disadvantage suffered by juveniles and their parents as compared with adult defendants who are entitled to see all reports about them presented to the court in criminal proceedings, but also one between the practice regarding SIRs the whole contents of which were generally revealed to parents and defendants, and school reports which were in the majority of courts regarded as confidential to the court (Ball, 1983). Having read any reports and heard any mitigation from a legal representative, or from unrepresented juveniles and parents, the court proceeds to sentence.

Orders in ascending order of severity
The following orders may be made in respect of children found guilty of criminal offences:

(a)   *A discharge*, which may be *absolute* or *conditional*, under which if the offender appears in court for a subsequent offence during the period of the condition (max. 3 years), he may be dealt with for the original offence as well as the current one.

(b)   *A fine*, subject to a limit of £100 for a child and £400 for a young person. Under section 26 of the Criminal Justice Act 1982, the parent or guardian is required to pay unless he cannot be found or it would be unreasonable to order him to do so having regard to the circumstances of the offence.

Supervision orders
There are five types of supervision order under the 1969 Act, as most recently amended by the Criminal Justice Act 1988, Part IX, and Schedule 10; orders may be for a maximum of 3 years:

1. A supervision order, to which may be added the require-
    ments to reside with a particular person who is agreeable
    (s.12(1)), or a requirement — provided that evidence re-
    quired under the Mental Health Act 1983 is available —
    to undergo medical treatment (s.12B).
2. A supervision order with a requirement under section
    12(2) to comply with directions given by the supervisor
    to undertake activities arranged by the supervisor. This
    provision under section 12(2) is known as 'intermediate
    treatment', although this term does not appear in the Act.
3. Under section 12A(3), a supervision order with a require-
    ment to undertake activities or to refrain from activities
    specified by the court.
4. Provided the defendant is of school age and the court
    having consulted the local authority is satisfied that
    arrangements exist for suitable education, and considers
    the order necessary to secure good conduct or prevent
    further offending, an order requiring the juvenile to
    comply with whatever arrangements for his education
    are made by his parents and approved by the education
    authority may be attached to a supervision order (s.12C).
5. In some circumstances, a court making a specified
    activities requirement under section 12A(3) may, pro-
    vided criteria similar to those justifying the use of a
    custodial sentence in the new section 1(4) and 1(4A) of
    the Criminal Justice Act 1982 are satisfied (see p. 112),
    must state in open court why it finds the criteria satis-
    fied and that it is making a supervision order instead of
    a custodial sentence (s.12D). This has implications if the
    order is breached (for further detail, see Stone, 1988).

As with supervision orders made in care proceedings, a
juvenile who fails to comply with the requirements in a
supervision order may be brought back to court on an
application by the local authority to discharge the supervision and replace it with a care order. Breach of any
requirement in a supervision order made in criminal proceedings, except under section 12B, may make a juvenile
liable for a fine of up to £100 or an Attendance Centre
order. However, if the court has stated that the supervision
order with specified requirements (s.12A(3)) was made
instead of a custodial sentence, the order may be discharged

and the court may order any disposal which could have been imposed for the original offence.

Attendance Centre orders   These orders may be made on 10–16-year-old boys and girls where Attendance Centres are available. The order may be for 12–24 hours, except that an offender under age 14 may be ordered less where 12 hours is considered excessive, and should not generally receive more than 12 hours. The order may be for up to 24 hours for 15–16-year-olds. The order requires the offender to attend at a centre, generally run by the police on Saturday afternoons, to participate in two hour sessions of physical and craft activities until the hours ordered have been completed.

Proof of breach of an order enables the offender to be dealt with in another way for the original offence. A new Attendance Centre order may be made while an existing one is running, regardless of the numbers of hours still to run.

Care order   The 1969 Act (s.7(7)) as amended by the Criminal Justice Act 1982 (s.23), following considerable research evidence of the abuse of care orders in criminal proceedings, inserted subsection 7(A) into section 7 (see Morris and Giller, 1987):

> s.7(7A)   A court shall not make a care order under subsection (7) of this section in respect of a child or young person unless it is of the opinion —
> (a) that a care order is appropriate because of the seriousness of the offence; and
> (b) that the child or young person is in need of care or control which he is unlikely to receive unless the court makes a care order.

Legal representation   A care order may not be made against an unrepresented juvenile unless he was refused legal aid because of his (or his parents') means, or he refused or failed to apply after being given the opportunity to do so. As care orders last (unless discharged) until the child is 18 years of age, the care order made in criminal proceedings is effectively an indeterminate sentence. This has long been the subject of criticism, and there is currently a fairly controversial consultative paper proposing the replacement of section 7(7) care orders with short determinate residential orders. Controversy mainly centres on the criteria for making the orders which many involved professionally see as being drafted unduly widely.

The power to add a condition as to the charge and control of an offender in care The Criminal Justice Act 1982 (s.22) provides for amendment of the Child Care Act 1980 (s.20), that if a juvenile already the subject of a care order made under section 7(7), or based on the offence condition in care proceedings, is found guilty of a further imprisonable offence, the court may restrict the local authorities' liberty to restore the care and control of the juvenile to his parents for up to 6 months (1980 Act, s.20(A)). The court may impose this restriction only if it considers that no other disposal is appropriate because of the seriousness of the offence, and for this purpose must obtain and consider information about the circumstances. The same legal representation restrictions apply as above.

The juvenile, parent and local authority may all apply to the court to vary or revoke the restriction. The local authority may appeal to the Crown Court against the addition or the terms of the restriction.

Community Service order

Under section 68 of the 1982 Act and Schedule 12, a Community Service order (CSO) may be made on a 16-year-old, subject to a maximum of 120 hours, provided he consents and the court is satisfied that a scheme exists for 16-year-olds and that the offender is a suitable candidate for such work and can be accommodated within the scheme.

Custodial sentences

Under the Criminal Justice Act 1988, a single sentence of detention in a young offender institution replaces Detention Centre and Youth Custody orders. This sentence will be available for boys aged 14–20 and girls aged 15–20. Efforts during the passage of the Bill to raise the age for liability to custody for boys to 15 years failed. It is still on the agenda of all concerned organizations (Children's Society, 1988).

Such sentences may be passed only if the court is satisfied, on grounds which must relate to the offender, that no other method of dealing with the defendant is appropriate because:

(a) he has a history of failure to respond to non-custodial penalties;
(b) no other sentence would be adequate to protect the public from serious harm;
(c) the offence was so serious that a non-custodial sentence cannot be justified (1988 Act, s.1(4)).

Implementation of this subsection will inevitably be followed by judicial decisions interpreting 'serious harm' and 'so serious' offences.

*Hospital or Guardianship order under
the Mental Health Act 1959*
This is very rarely used. Hospital or Guardianship orders under the Mental Health Act 1983, section 37, are very occasionally used where the offence is imprisonable in the case of an adult and the court has medical evidence that the child is suffering from mental illness, psychopathic disorder or severe mental impairment. A Hospital order can only be made if the condition is treatable and Guardianship orders are only available to the Juvenile Court for children of age 16 years.

Additional orders
The Juvenile Court can impose other orders in addition to disposal.

1. *Compensation* Under section 67 of the Criminal Justice Act 1982, compensation to the victim for damage or injury may be awarded either in addition to, or instead of, another disposal. If the offender's means are insufficient to pay a fine and compensation, the court must give preference to compensation.
2. Costs.
3. Deprivation of property used for criminal purposes.

Pressure for change

It is generally accepted that custody for juveniles is damaging and, as reconviction rates following any custodial sentence are uniformly high (75–80 per cent), ineffective. Over recent years considerable progress has been achieved by local authority social service departments and the probation service, working with the police, to reduce the number of juveniles appearing in court. Both the agencies and the voluntary sector have also, encouraged by funding resulting from a DHSS initiative in 1983, provided community-based programmes which have been widely used by courts as an alternative to custodial sentences, and have contributed significantly to the overall reduction of custodial sentences for juveniles from 7,000 in 1981 to 4,400 in 1986 (NACRO, 1987). However, geographical comparisons show that there are a number of areas dealing with similar offenders committing similar offences in which custody rates are still very high.

Recently a Children's Society Advisory Committee, on which most of the professional groups working with young offenders were represented, has set an agenda for the future by calling for the abolition of all penal custody for juveniles. The committee's report recognizes that while practice in many areas has shown that most serious offenders (who elsewhere are sent to custody) can be involved in community-based programmes, there will always be a small minority (estimated at approx. 350 per year) for whom secure residential provision outside the penal system is the only solution (Children's Society, 1988).

Bibliography

Adcock, M., White, R. and Rowland, O. (1983), *The Administrative Parent — a Study of the Assumption of Parental Rights and Duties*, London: BAAF.

Alison, N. (1980), *Rights and Risks*, London: National Corporation for the Care of Old People.

Anderson, R. (1978), *Representation in the Juvenile Court*, London: Routledge and Kegan Paul.

Ball, C. (1981a), 'The use and significance of school reports in Juvenile Court criminal proceedings: a research note', *British Journal of Social Work*, 11(4), 479–83.

Ball, C. (1981b), 'Minor motoring offences committed by juveniles: the case for allowing a guilty plea by letter', *Justice of the Peace*, 145, 10.

Ball, C. (1983), 'Secret justice: the use made of school reports in juvenile courts', *British Journal of Social Work*, 13(2), 197–206.

Ball, C. (1986a), 'Legal eye', *Community Care*, 22.7.86, p. 15.

Ball, C. (1986b), 'Legal eye', *Community Care*, 30.10.86, p. 12.

Ball, C. (1987a), 'Legal eye', *Community Care*, 22.10.87, p. 13.

Ball, C. (1987b), 'Legal representation for the child in adoption proceedings', *Family Law*, 17, 230.

Ball, C. (1987c), *Social Work Law File: Child Care Law*, Monograph, UEA, Norwich.

Ball, C. (1987d), 'Legal eye', *Community Care*, 5.3.87, p. 18.

Ball, C. (1988a), 'Legal eye', *Community Care*, 25.2.88, p. 20.

Ball, C. (1988b), 'Legal eye', *Community Care*, 23.9.88, p. 12.

Ball, C., Harris, R., Roberts, G. and Vernon, S. (1988), *The Law Report: Teaching and Assessment of Law in Social Work Education*, London: CCETSW.

Barnard, D. (1988), *The Criminal Court in Action*, 3rd edn, London: Butterworths.

Blom-Cooper, L. (1985), *A Child in Trust: The Report of the Panel of Inquiry into the Circumstances Surrounding the Death of Jasmine Beckford*, London: London Borough of Brent.

Blom-Cooper, L. (1987), *A Child in Mind: The Report of the Commission of Inquiry into the Circumstances Surrounding the Death of Kimberley Carlile*, London: London Borough of Greenwich.

Bottomley, A.K. (1973), *Decisions in the Penal Process*, London: Martin Robertson.

Bottoms, A. (1974), 'On the decriminalisation of the English Juvenile Courts' in R. Hood (ed.), *Crime, Criminology and Public Policy*, London: Heinemann, pp. 319–46.

Bromley, P.M. and Lowe, N.V. (1987), *Family Law*, 7th edn, London: Butterworths.

Butler, Lord (1975), *Report of the Committee on Mentally Abnormal Offenders*, Cmnd 6244, London: HMSO.

Butler-Sloss, Dame Elizabeth (1988), *Report of the Inquiry into Child Abuse in Cleveland*, Cmnd 412, London: HMSO.

CCETSW (1974), *Legal Studies in Social Work Education*, Social Work Curriculum Study Paper 4, London: CCETSW.

CCETSW (1987), *Regulations and Guidance for the Training of Social Workers to be Considered for Approval in England and Wales under the Mental Health Act 1983*, Paper 19.19, London: CCETSW.

Child Care Law Review (CCLR) (1985), *Child Care Law Review*, London: DHSS.

Clarke, D. (1987), *Safeguarding Children — a Procedural Guide to the Work of the Guardian ad Litem in Care Proceedings*, Rye, Kent and Sussex Independent Counselling Agency.

Clulow, C. and Vincent, C. (1987), *In the Child's Best Interests*, London: Tavistock.

Cretney, S. (1984), *Principles of Family Law*, 4th edn, London: Sweet and Maxwell.

Davies, M. (1985), *The Essential Social Worker*, 2nd edn, Aldershot: Gower.

DHSS (1976), *A Review of the Mental Health Act 1959*, London: HMSO.

DHSS (1986), *Secure Accommodation (No. 2) (Amendment) Regulations*, LAC/86/13, London: HMSO.

DHSS (1987), *The Law on Child Care and Family Services*, Cmnd 62, London: HMSO.

DHSS (1988), *Panel Administration: A Guide to the Administration of Panels of Guardians ad Litem and Reporting Officers*, London: DHSS.

DHSS (annual), *A Guide to Non Contributory Benefit for Disabled People*, Leaflet HB5, London: DHSS.

Disability Alliance (annual), *Disability Rights Handbook*, 25 Denmark Street, London WC2H 8NJ.

Dyde, W. (1986), *Place of Safety Orders*, Norwich: University of East Anglia Social Work Monographs No. 52.

Freeman, M.D.A. (1986), *Law and Practice of Custodianship*, London: Sweet and Maxwell.

Gostin, L. (1975), *A Human Condition: The Mental Health Act from 1959 to 1975: Observations, Analysis and Proposals for Reform*, London: MIND, Vol. 1.

Gostin, L. (1978), *The Great Debate: MIND's Comments on the White Paper; The Review of the Mental Health Act 1959*, London: MIND.

Gostin, L., Meacher, M. and Olsen, M.R. (1983), *The Mental Health Act 1983: a Guide for Social Workers*, Birmingham: BASW.

Hilgendorf, L. (1981), *Social Workers and Solicitors in Child Care Cases*, London: HMSO.

HMSO (1966), *Legal Aid in Criminal Proceedings* (Widgery Report), Cmnd 2934, London: HMSO.

HMSO (1978), *The Report of the Committee of Enquiry into the Education of Handicapped Children and Young People* (Warnock Report), Cmnd 7212, London: HMSO.

HMSO (1984), *Second Report of the Social Services Committee (1983–4): Children in Care* (Short Report), HC 360-I.

HMSO (1986), *22nd Report of the Criminal Injuries Compensation Board*, Cmnd 42, London: HMSO.

Hoath, D.C. (1983), *Homelessness*, London: Sweet and Maxwell.

Hoggett, B. (1984), *Mental Health Law*, 2nd edn, London: Sweet and Maxwell.

Hoggett, B. (1987), *Parents and Children: The Law of Parental Responsibility*, 3rd edn, London: Sweet and Maxwell.

Home Office (1979), Home Office Circular 138/79.

Home Office (1985), *Code of Practice for the Identification of Persons by Police Officers*, London: HMSO.

Jackson, S. (1987), *The Education of Children in Care*, Bristol Papers in Applied Social Studies, University of Bristol.

Judicial Statistics (1986), London: HMSO.

Lakhani, B., Luba, J., Ravetz, A., Read, J. and Wood, P. (1988), *National Welfare Benefits Handbook*, London: CPAG.

Law Commission (1987a), *Care, Supervision and Interim Orders in Custody Proceedings*, Working Paper 100, London: HMSO.

Law Commission (1987b), *Wards of Court*, Working Paper No. 101, London: HMSO.

Liell, P. and Saunders, J.B. (1987), *The Law of Education*, 9th edn, London: Butterworths.

Lowe, N.V. and White, R. (1986), *Wards of Court*, 2nd edn, London: Barry Rose.

Lustgarten, L. (1980), *Legal Control of Racial Discrimination*, London: Macmillan.

McDonnell, P. and Aldgate, J. (1984), *Reviews of Children in Care*, Barnett House Papers, Oxford.

Masson, J. and Shaw, M. (1988), 'The work of guardians ad litem', *Journal of Social Welfare Law*, 3, 164–84.

Millham, S., Bullock, R., Hosie, K. and Haak, M. (1986), *Lost in Care: The Problems of Maintaining Links between Children in Care and their Families*, Aldershot: Gower.

Moeran, E. (1982), *Practical Legal Aid*, London: Oyez Longman.

Morris, A. and Giller, H. (1987), *Understanding Juvenile Justice*, London: Croom Helm.

Morris, A., Giller, H., Szwed, E. and Geach, H. (1980), *Justice for Children*, London: Macmillan.

Murch, M. (1980), *Justice and Welfare in Divorce*, London: Sweet and Maxwell.

Murch, M. (1984), *Separate Representation for Parents and*

Children: An Examination of the Initial Phase, Family Law Research Unit, University of Bristol.

NACRO (1984), *School Reports in the Juvenile Court*, London: NACRO.

NACRO (1987), *Time for Change: Report of the Juvenile Crime Advisory Committee*, London: NACRO.

NACRO (1988a), *Grave Crimes: Grave Doubts: Report of the NACRO Working Group on Sentences Made under s.53 of the Children and Young Persons Act 1933*, London: NACRO.

NACRO (1988b), *School Reports: A Second Look*, London: NACRO.

Packman, J., with Randall, J. and Jacques, N. (1986), *Who Needs Care? Social Work Decisions about Children*, Oxford: Basil Blackwell.

Pannick, D. (1985), *Sex Discrimination Law*, Oxford: Clarendon Press.

Parker, H., Casburn, M. and Turnbull, D. (1981), *Receiving Juvenile Justice*, Oxford: Basil Blackwell.

Pearce, N. (1984), *Adoption Practice and Procedure*, London: Format.

Pearce, N. (1986), *Custodianship: The Law and Practice*, London: Format.

Priestley, P., Fears, D. and Fuller, R. (1977), *Justice for Juveniles*, London: Routledge and Kegan Paul.

Rashid, S.O. and Ball, C. (1987), *Social Work Law File: Mental Health, Disability, Homelessness and Race Relations*, Monograph, UEA, Norwich.

Rowland, M. (1988), *Rights Guide to Non-Means-Tested Social Security Benefits*, London: CPAG.

Sinclair, R. (1984), *Decision Making in Statutory Reviews on Children in Care*, Aldershot: Gower.

Stone, K. (1987), *The Statementing Process*, Social Work Monograph No. 51, UEA, Norwich.

Stone, N. (1988), *Social Work Law File: Probation Law*, Monograph, UEA, Norwich.

Stone, N. (1989), *Social Work Law File: Court Welfare Law*, Monograph, UEA, Norwich.

Street, H. and Brazier, R. (1986), *De Smith on Constitutional and Administrative Law*, 5th edn, Harmondsworth: Penguin.

Sumner, M., Jarvis, J. and Parker, H. (1988), 'Objective or

objectionable: school reports in the Juvenile Court', *Youth and Policy*, 23, 14–18.

Thoburn, J. (1988), *Child Placement: Principles and Practice*, Aldershot: Gower.

Thorpe, D., Smith, D., Green, C. and Paley, J. (1980), *Out of Care: The Community Support of Juvenile Offenders*, London: Allen and Unwin.

Tinker, A. (1985), *The Elderly in Modern Society*, 2nd edn, London: Longman.

Tutt, N. and Giller, H. (1983), 'Police cautioning of juveniles: the practice of diversity', *Criminal Law Review*, 587–95.

Vernon, J. and Fruin, D. (1986), *In Care: A Study of Social Work Decision Making*, London: National Children's Bureau.

Walker, N. (1985), *Sentencing: Theory, Law and Practice*, London: Butterworths.

Zander, M. (1986), *Police and Criminal Evidence Act 1984*, London: Sweet and Maxwell.

Glossary of legal terms

Affidavit	Written statement made for the purposes of proceedings and signed and sworn or affirmed before an authorized official.
Certiorari	Order of the High Court to review and quash the decision of a lower court which was based on an irregular procedure.
Cross-examination	Questions put to a witness by other parties to test out evidence given.
Discovery of documents	Disclosure of documents to other parties before proceedings.
Estoppel	A rule which prevents a person denying the truth of a statement or the existence of facts which that person has led another to believe.
Examination 'in chief'	The interrogation by a witness by those who have called him.
Ex parte	Application made by one party in the absence of other parties (e.g. place of safety orders).
Functus officio	The position of a person who having had authority to act has discharged it and is no longer authorized to act.
Guardian ad litem	Guardian for the duration of the legal proceedings.
Hearsay evidence	Evidence of facts in issue which are not within the direct knowledge of the witness, but have been communicated to him by another.
Indictment	Written accusation charging a Crown Court defendant.

Injunction	Court order requiring someone to do or refrain from doing something.
Inter partes	Proceedings in which all parties are heard.
Interim	Literally 'in the meantime', an order made before the full hearing.
Lacuna	A gap in the law.
Leading question	Question suggesting the required answer, or one which can only be answered 'yes' or 'no'.
Mandamus	Command from the High Court to a lower court to do what is required.
Mens rea	The guilty intention to commit a crime.
Next friend	The person through whom a minor or mental health patient acts in legal proceedings.
Obiter dictum	Statement of opinion by a judge which is not directly relevant to the case being tried.
Plaintiff	The person who brings a civil action.
Prohibition	Order of the High Court preventing a lower court from exceedings its jurisdiction or acting contrary to the rules of natural justice.
Putative father	The man alleged to be the father of an illegitimate child.
Ratio decidendi	The reason for a judicial decision.
Re-examination	Questions put to the witness by the person calling him after cross-examination.
Statutory instrument	Subordinate legislation made in exercise of a power granted by statute.
Sub judice	During the course of a legal trial or under consideration.
Subpoena	Court order that a person attends court to give evidence or to produce documents.
Ultra vires	An act outside the authority conferred by law.

Name index

Adcock, M., 60
Aldgate, J., 73
Alison, N., 99
Anderson, R., 101

Ball, C., xiii, 11, 17, 32, 47, 66,
    78, 87, 89, 94, 98, 99, 101,
    105, 107, 108
Barnard, D., 49
Blom-Cooper, L., 55, 65, 66, 68
Bottomley, K., 48
Bottoms, A., 54
Brazier, R., 11
Bromley, P., 13, 23, 75
Butler, R., 93
Butler-Sloss, E., 55, 66, 67, 82

Casburn, M., 101
Clarke, D., 82
Clulow, C., 18
Cretney, S., 13, 70

Davies, M., xii
Dyde, W., 66

Fears, D., 101, 104
Freeman, M., 78
Fruin, D., 58, 60, 73
Fuller, R., 101, 104

Giller, H., 101, 105, 110
Gostin, L., 87, 93

Hilgendorf, L., 102

Hoath, D., 28
Hoggett, B., 57, 78, 84, 87, 89,
    92, 93, 94, 97

Jackson, S., 72

Lakhani, B., 38, 39, 40
Liell, P., 32
Lowe, N., 13, 23, 70, 75, 84
Lustgarten, L., 40

Olsen, M., 87
Ormrod, Lord, 54

Packman, J., 58, 60, 61, 67
Pannick, D., 40
Parker, H., 101
Pearce, N., 75, 78
Priestley, P., 101, 104

Rashid, S., 87, 89, 94, 99
Rowland, M., 35, 36, 37
Rowland, O., 60

Saunders, J., 32
Shaw, M., 62
Sinclair, R., 73
Stone, K., 33
Stone, N., 49, 95
Street, H., 11
Sumner, M., 107

Thoburn, J., 70, 73, 80
Thorpe, D., 106

Tinker, A., 99
Turnbull, D., 101
Tutt, N., 105

Vernon, J., 58, 60, 73
Vincent, C., 18

Waite, Mr Justice, 54
Walker, N., 49
Warnock, Baroness, 32
White, R., 60, 70, 84
Widgery, Lord, 9

Zander, M., 42, 48

Index

Access
  children in care 72–3
  DHSS Code of Practice 72
  juvenile court orders 72
  matrimonial proceedings 18
  termination of 72
  white paper proposals 73
Adoption
  care orders and, 56, 77
  custodianship as alternative
    79
  freeing for adoption 77–8
  guardian ad litem 76
  procedure 76
  Schedule 2 report 75
  step-parent by, 77
Appeals
  care proceedings 63
  civil proceedings 7
  criminal proceedings 6
Approved social workers 87

BAAF 54
Bail 48

Care
  assumption of parental rights
    58–60, 70
  local authority's duty 58, 69
  parental access 72–3
  placement in, 70–72
  voluntary admission 57, 69
  reviews of children in, 73

secure accommodation 54,
    70–71
Care orders
  care proceedings in, 62
  criminal proceedings in, 110–
    11
  'exceptional circumstances'
    70
Care proceedings
  appeals 63
  care or control test 61
  duty to investigate 61
  grandparents in, 63–4
  grounds 61
  guardian ad litem 62–3
  orders in, 62–3
  parents as parties 62
  procedure 62–3
  reports 62
CCETSW xii, 89
Child Poverty Action Group 34,
    37, 38, 39
Children
  'child of the family' 15, 17–
    18, 24
  custody orders 18–19
  guardianship of children 16,
    56
  in care 56
  welfare principle 18–19, 72,
    76, 79, 80
Children's Legal Centre 70
Children's Society 111, 113

125

Citizens arrest 45
Civil Law 3
Cleveland Inquiry 55, 66
Committees of Inquiry
    Jasmine Beckford 55
    Kimberley Carlile 55, 65, 67
'Community Care' 34
Commission for Racial Equality
    40
Court of Protection 97–8
Court Welfare Officer 18
Courts
    civil 4, 6
    County Court 5, 6, 13, 16,
        23, 27, 76, 79, 82
    Court of Appeal 5, 6, 7
    criminal 4, 7
    Crown Court 5, 6, 7, 49, 63
    Divisional Court 7, 63
    Domestic Court 6, 16, 24, 76,
        79, 82
    European Court 6, 70
    Family Division 6, 64
    High Court 6, 13, 16, 27, 76,
        79, 82
    House of Lords 5, 6, 72
    Juvenile Court 5, 31, 56, 71,
        72, 73
    Magistrates Court 5, 7, 31, 48
CQSW xii
Custodianship
    alternative to adoption 78–9
    application by carers 80
    care order on revocation 56
    effect of order 78
    reports in proceedings 79
    welfare test 79

Disability Alliance 34, 37
Disabled people
    assessment of need 98
    register of, 98
    welfare benefits for 36–7
Discrimination
    racial 40
    sexual 40

Divorce
    'child of the family' 15–16,
        18
    decree absolute 15
    decree nisi 15
    financial provision 15
    grounds 14
    matrimonial home 19–20
    petition 13–14
    'special procedure' 14
Domestic violence
    accommodation for victims
        20, 21
    children's needs 21–2
    injunctions 22–3
    personal protection 22
    power of arrest 23, 24

Education
    care proceedings 31–2
    education welfare officers 31
    'free' schools 32
    learning difficulty 32
    school attendance 31–2
    special educational needs
        32–3
    'statementing' 33
    Warnock report 32–3
Elderly people
    compulsory removal from
        home 99
    Part III accommodation 98
Emergency protection
    definition of place of safety
        66
    emergency protection orders
        67
    entry warrants 64–5
    place of safety orders 65–7
    police detention 67–8
Equal Opportunities Com-
    mission 40
Evidence
    affidavit 84, 120
    best evidence 10
    cross examination 120

examination in chief 120
hearsay evidence 10, 120
leading questions 10–11
standard of proof 10
subpoena 121

Glossary 120–121
Guardian ad litem
    access proceedings, in 72
    adoption proceedings, in 76
    care proceedings, in 62
    definition 120
Guardianship
    access for grandparents 16
    applications 16–17
    putative fathers' applications
        17
    welfare principle 17–18

Homelessness
    definition 28
    intentional homelessness 28
    judicial review of decisions 30
    local connection 30
    priority need 29–30
Hospital order
    care proceedings, in 63
    criminal proceedings, in 96
Housing
    eviction 26–7
    harrassment 27–8
    injunctions 27–8
    occupation 25–6
    unlawful eviction 27–8

Injunction 21, 22, 27, 121

Judges Rules 41
Judicial precedent
    definition 5
    hierarchy of the courts 3
    obiter dictum 121
    ratio decidendi 121
Judicial Review
    as means of appeal 30
    breach of natural justice 11, 12

orders,
    certiorari 120
    mandamus 121
    prohibition 121
    ultra vires 121
Jury 7
Justice of the Peace 64, 100
Juvenile Court
    advance information 105
    constitution 101–102
    jurisdiction,
        civil 102–3
        criminal 103
    orders,
        attendance centre 110
        care order 110–11
        community service 111
        compensation 112
        costs 112
        custodial sentences 111–
            13
        deprivation of property
            112
        discharges 108
        fine 108
        supervision order 108–110
    press reports 105
    procedure 105–106
    reports,
        school 107
        social inquiry 106–107
        'stand down' 107
    separation from adult courts
        102
    'welfare of the child' 105
Juvenile offenders
    age of criminal responsibility
        103
    alternatives to custody 112
    'appropriate adult' 46, 103–
        104
    arrest of, 104
    cautioning 104–105
    certified 'unruly' 104
    fingerprints 47
    interviews at school 103

Juvenile offenders (cont.)
  legal advice 104
  legal aid 104
  remand, in care 104

Lacuna 121
Law Commission 16, 55, 80, 81, 84
Law Society, child care panel 8
Legal Action Group 39
Legal Aid
  advice and representation 8
  civil 8, 9
  criminal 8-9
  'green form' scheme 8-9
  Widgery criteria 9
Legal profession
  barristers 8
  judges 3
  solicitors 8

'McKenzie man' 9
Mental disorder
  approved social worker 89, 90, 91, 92, 94
  compulsory powers,
    assessment 90-91
    assessment in an emergency 91-2
    detention in place of safety 93
    patients in hospital 93
    treatment 92-3
  consent to treatment 92-3
  court of protection 97-8
  court orders,
    hospital 96
    interim 95
    remand, report 95
    remand, treatment 95
    restriction order 96
  definitions of mental illness 88
  guardianship 94
  Mental Health Review
    Tribunal 91, 93, 96-7

MIND 93
  responsible medical officer 92, 93
  voluntary treatment 87-8

NACRO 101, 102, 103, 107, 108, 113
National Insurance 34-5
Natural justice 12
NSPCC 62

Ombudsman 11

Police
  arrest 43-5
  caution 47
  Codes of Practice 41
  Custody officer 46
  detention 45-6
  fingerprints 47
  juveniles 46-7
  search warrants 43
  'stop and search' 42-3
Poor law 54
Putative father 16, 17

Reporting Officer 76

Secure accommodation 54
Statutory instrument 121
Subjudice 121
Supervision orders
  care proceedings 73-4
  criminal proceedings 74, 108-110
  discharge 74
  requirements in, 74

Tribunals 11

Wardship
  committal to care 56
  common law jurisdiction 81
  definition 80
  incidence of use 81

local authority, use by 63, 81–4
origination summons 81
'safety net', use as 75
secure accommodation 70–71
sterilization, and 82
'stop list' 82
Welfare benefits
   child benefit 35

claims 37
contributory 35
disabled, for 36–7
income related
   family credit 37–40
   housing benefit 39
   income support 38
   social fund 39–40